Prentice-Hall, Inc., Englewood Cliffs, N. J.

Traditional

Exchange

and

Modern

Markets

CYRIL S. BELSHAW   The University of British Columbia

Library of Congress Catalog Card No.: 65-23229

Printed in the United States of America
C-92610(C)   C-92609(P)

TO DIANA

PRENTICE-HALL INTERNATIONAL, INC.
London

PRENTICE-HALL OF AUSTRALIA, PTY., LTD.
Sydney

PRENTICE-HALL OF CANADA, LTD.
Toronto

PRENTICE-HALL OF INDIA (PRIVATE) LTD.
New Delhi

PRENTICE-HALL OF JAPAN, INC.
Tokyo

WILBERT E. MOORE / NEIL J. SMELSER   Editors

Modernization of Traditional Societies Series

The twentieth century will be called many
things by future historians—the Age of Global
War, perhaps, the Age of Mass Society,
the Age of the Psychoanalytic Revolution,
to name a few possibilities. One name that
historians certainly will not fail to give
our century is the Age of the New Nation. For,
evidently, the convulsive emergence of
the colonies into independence and their
subsequent struggle to join the ranks of the
prosperous, powerful, and peaceful is the
most remarkable revolution of our time.
Taking the world as a whole, men are now
preoccupied with no subject more than they
are with the travail of the New Nations.
The world of the social sciences
has been studying the pace of social
change in these newly emergent areas,
and from time to time has been engaging in
technical assistance and even in the giving
of advice on high levels of social strategy.
Little of this effort has reached publicly
accessible form. Though technical treatises
abound, and isolated, journalistic reports
of distinctly exotic countries are not
wanting, college curricula have scarcely
reflected either the scientific endeavors or
the world-wide revolutions in technology
and in political affairs.
This series on "Modernization of
Traditional Societies" is designed to
inform scholars, students, and citizens about
the way quiet places have come alive, and
to introduce at long last materials on
EDITORIAL   FOREWORD   the contemporary character of

developing areas into college curricula for the thought leaders of the near future. To these ends we have assembled experts over the range of the social sciences and over the range of the areas of the underdeveloped and newly developing sections of the earth that were once troublesome only to themselves.

We are proud to be participants in this series, and proud to offer each of its volumes to the literate world, with the hope that that world may increase, prosper, think, and decide wisely.

WILBERT E. MOORE
NEIL J. SMELSER

My aim has been to compare several kinds of economy, from the primitive to the modern, to show the themes they have in common and their differences, and to indicate the principles of modernization that new nations are attempting to follow. I have tried to do this in a way which brings economic, anthropological, and sociological ideas together, since in my view these disciplines should constitute one system.

This is a rapidly growing field of study, with a short history and a long future. I have tried to sort out the various theoretical approaches and bring them together or give reasons for discarding them as the case may be, and to indicate sources for their further study. But as theoretical ideas change, new questions arise for answering: I believe it to be an important task for a book such as this to raise those questions, and to suggest inquiry perhaps by stimulating

PREFACE   disagreement as well as agreement.—CYRIL S. BELSHAW

Contents

In popular and scholarly thought alike, the fundamental characteristic of a developed society is a complex and dynamic economy. However, many of the new nations engaged in the task of rapid modernization are handicapped on the one hand by a lack of developed wealth, and on the other by the lack of a well-integrated economy oriented towards rapid growth. There are many conceptual problems underlying the analysis of this situation and the steps that might be taken to correct it. Many of them turn upon a presumed interrelationship between the economic system and the social and cultural context in which it works. It has been argued, for example, that economic individualism is a necessary condition for economic progress, since individualism provides the motivations upon which determined effort can be based. If this social premise is accepted, it leads to the notion that the individual family characteristic of Western society is a more appropriate base for economic growth than the extended kinship systems of some African and Asian countries. Hence such a country, faced with the task of modernization, should first of all alter the basis of its family life. This example of individualism is an inaccurate oversimplification of one complex social factor which must be analyzed before an adequate picture of social, cultural, and economic interrelations can be achieved. The rapid growth of new nations has led to the examination of the growth of income and

Economy and Society

wealth in a context of widely variable cultures and social structures.

At first there was concern about the social consequences of economic growth, seen in such terms as family change, urbanization, and political development. Then attention was given to the social concomitants of economic growth, on the assumption that there was an interplay and mutual influence between society and economy. This, of course, was not a new idea, since it had formed the basis of much of the writing of Adam Smith, Alfred Marshall, Marx and Veblen, and those anthropologists who interested themselves in economics. But the growth of formal economic theory had tended to exclude examinations of the social variables until cross-cultural comparisons reinforced their relevance. And in the past few years another step has been taken. We now hear of the social prerequisites to economic growth. The Marxian idea that something economic determines forms of society has been modified by the notion that certain social and cultural forms may be necessary before economic growth can take place.

Whatever the theories may be explicitly, they imply an interrelationship between an economy and a society, or at least between something economic and something social. It is then at least reasonable to assume that the entities to be interrelated are identifiable or observable. Although economists have not on the whole attempted to define the economy, it is not difficult to infer what they would delineate, basing the inference on their approach to the subject matter of economics.

One departure point is that the economy has to do with those actions and institutions which are related to the wealth of the society. This premise can lead directly to an approach which integrates society and economy, as was the case with Adam Smith and much of the writing of Alfred Marshall, on the assumption that *all* institutions have something to do with wealth. Marshall, indeed, described economics as the study of mankind "in the ordinary business of life," [1] which makes the economy life as a whole.

Others see a dilemma in this position, and in order to escape it introduce the idea that wealth is material, or that it is useful and exchangeable. The idea that wealth is only material is not strictly supportable, since at the very least we are concerned with services of a nonmaterial kind. To define entertainment or health services out of the economy would be arbitrary, and computations of national income always include them. And if this is done, we should treat ceremonial and witchcraft in the same light. To think of wealth as being useful and exchangeable is more acceptable, and leads directly to the position that exchange

---

[1] Alfred Marshall, *Principles of Economics* (London: Macmillan & Co., Ltd., 1898).

and the market are the central features of the economy, which is indeed a central theme of the present study.

Another school of thought, led by A. C. Pigou, refers to those activities which can be related to the measuring rod of money. This operational approach is a sharpening of the "useful exchange" idea, since money cannot be used to measure unless there is the potentiality of exchange, and exchange will not take place unless there is utility. It should be stressed here, since this is most important in the cross-cultural comparison of economic systems, that usefulness or utility refers not to some objective criterion of technical effectiveness but to the purely subjective notion of the actor that the good or service is valuable to him, or that he wants it. Why he wants it (for aesthetic or pleasurable reasons, because of religious or secular values) is quite irrelevant to the notion of utility. This usage of economists should be carried over into anthropology and sociology.

The measuring rod of money is a precise and useful criterion for economists to apply when they are examining their own society, and in fact most economists use it. It leads to skilled technical analysis of the price mechanism, markets, and certain forms of production and consumption. But this is at a cost of a considerable difficulty which inhibits our ability to handle the problems of developing societies. One part of the difficulty is that many similar kinds of activities (for example, extensive subsistence agriculture with distribution through kinship networks rather than through buying and selling) take place in developing economies outside the influence of money, and we would be out of step in talking of primitive economies if, by money, we mean the kind of cash exchange and bank balances typical of capitalism. The other part of the difficulty is that the type of analysis which results does not admit of a ready linkage with sociology, so that social and cultural variables have to be abruptly put aside. This is altogether too ethnocentric a conception for us to use here.

A third starting point is to consider the system of production, distribution (exchange), and consumption. Among modern writers, Kenneth Boulding, for example, starts here. He points out [2] that these are the spheres of activity with which economists are primarily concerned. In further elaboration, he shows that the production and consumption activities of interest to the economist usually relate to exchange: "Indeed, it is hardly too much to say that the study of exchange comprises nine-tenths of the economist's dominion." An exception might be the study of the way in which entrepreneurs combine land, labor, and capi-

[2] Kenneth Boulding, *Economic Analysis* (New York: Harper & Row, Publishers, 1941), pp. 3-8.

tal which are already under their control and some of which they may not buy on the open market, but even here the conceptual tools are made possible by real or hypothetical exchange situations, and particularly by pricing and monetary evaluation.

This links with the most ambitious and sophisticated approach to the theoretical differentiation of economy and society, namely that of Talcott Parsons and Neil Smelser.[3] This is an elaboration and application of Parsons' general view that all social systems must contain functional subsystems. The economy is the adaptive subsystem. But whereas Boulding focuses on exchange, Parsons and Smelser make production the criterion, and define the economy as producing any of the wants which may be relevant to the society. Having produced them, it makes them available for the use of other subsystems within the society.[4] Had Parsons and Smelser taken exchange as the criterion of the economy they would, as sociologists, have had some difficulty in making the economy a differentiated part of the society. For it could be argued (as I shall argue in this volume) that all enduring social relations involve transactions, which have an exchange aspect.

We may now turn to another view of the economy which can be derived from the writings of economists who would see economics as being concerned with a special point of view about all action. The clearest exposition of this is in Lionel Robbins' *An Essay on the Nature and Significance of Economic Science*,[5] although Robbins confines himself to a discussion with economists and does not attempt to consider the implications for sociology or anthropology. The latter task is done for economic anthropology by Raymond Firth, and is consistent with the position taken by Talcott Parsons in *The Structure of Social Action*.

The much-quoted definition of Robbins must be stated again.

Economics is the science which studies human behavior as a relationship between ends and scarce means which have alternative uses.[6]

Since there has been some confusion as to the implications of this statement, let me give examples of Robbins' own illustrations, amended to fit our cross-cultural analysis of modernization.

---

[3] Talcott Parsons and Neil Smelser, *Economy and Society* (London: Routledge & Kegan Paul, Ltd., 1956).

[4] *Ibid.*, 24-25.

[5] Lionel Robbins, *An Essay on the Nature and Significance of Economic Science* (London: Macmillan & Co., Ltd., 1937).

[6] *Ibid.*, p. 16. The remaining quotations are drawn from the pages immediately preceding and following.

We do not say that the production of potatoes [rice, yams] is economic activity and the production of philosophy [Buddhist religion, ceremonial satisfactions] is not. We say rather that, insofar as either kind of activity involves the relinquishment of other desired alternatives, it has its economic aspect.

And, again:

But when time and the means for achieving ends are limited *and* capable of alternative application, *and* the ends are capable of being distinguished in order of importance, then behavior necessarily assumes the form of choice. Every act which involves time and scarce means for the achievement of one end involves the relinquishment of their use for the achievement of another. It has an economic aspect. If I want bread and sleep, and in the time at my disposal I cannot have all I want of both, then some part of my wants of bread and sleep must go unsatisfied. If, in a limited lifetime, I would wish to be both a philosopher and a mathematician [or a canoe builder and a clerk of a Native Authority and a politician], but my rate of acquisition of knowledge is such that I cannot do both completely, then some part of my wish for philosophical or mathematical competence or both must be relinquished.

Raymond Firth makes this problem of choice (within a framework of cultural imperatives) a central issue of social organization. If one starts with this kind of assumption, actions are not economic or noneconomic. There are not separable categories of economic acts and social acts. All acts have an economic aspect and a social and cultural aspect. But how can acts, whether of individuals or of corporate groups acting together, be shown to be interconnected if we are looking merely at aspects of them? There are two answers to this question.

The economic answer is that actions in a social context involve exchange. Exchange becomes that aspect of behavior which provides interconnections between individual acts of choice, and the possibility of institutionalized mechanisms of adjustment, such as price reactions. The actions of an isolated man can be subjected to economic analysis, but an economy is a system which gains reality through the social phenomenon of exchange.

The second answer to the problem of interconnectedness lies within the sphere of social and cultural analysis. Action is goal-oriented: that which the economist calls ends or wants, the sociologist calls goals. The selection of goals implies a choice, which in turn implies some psychological mechanism for evaluating goals and judging the costs of achieving them. But choice is not random. It is influenced by the processes which produce a value system for a culture, and it is made within the context of such a value system. Thus the economic interconnectedness of actions is based upon a premise of a value system produced by cultural processes (the anthropological theme in action).

A value system implies a spectrum of values which may in some respects be contradictory or competitive or dysfunctional, but which nevertheless is produced through the interplay between individual and culture. Within this spectrum certain regularities emerge which govern the formation of social roles, and the relationship between such roles. A system of roles, or a social structure, provides a further major framework which circumscribes action and describes forms of interconnectedness between actions. Once again, economic interconnectedness is based upon a premise of a social structure (the sociological theme in action).

EXCHANGE AND MARKETS

If we wish to understand the economic foundations of development, and to relate cultural and social analysis to them, we can do no better than to begin with the institutions of exchange. If we do, we will find that our examination touches in one way or another upon all spheres of social life, both empirically and analytically.

As a specific institution, exchange penetrates through the social fabric and may be thought of as a network holding society together. This applies whether we think of an isolated family group, the members of which give each other support and the benefit of differentiated services; or of an Oceanic culture in which reciprocal services and obligations link together in reflection of social structure and values; or of modern capitalism or communism in which exchange is rationalized by reference to a price system. In a very real sense, alterations in the economy, and hence economic development, consist in an alteration in the system of exchange. Economic growth (an increase in per capita income or wealth) is usually based upon institutional changes, of which the growing complexity and sophistication of the exchange system is the major index.

Similarly, if the term social development is to have any meaning, it must refer to an increase in social scale and an alteration in the quality of social institutions. Both these vague concepts refer to an increased complexity in the network of institutional and role relationships. Increased complexity must be based upon increased division of labor. And if there is increased division of labor, with institutions or role players dividing up more and more tasks, more and more services and goods will be provided for others. This means that there will be an increase in the total exchange system of a society. The exchange system is merely one aspect of the regularities of social relationships.[7]

There are thus as many exchange systems as there are types of society, for they are fundamentally coterminous. It is not the purpose of this study to provide a typology, since it is doubtful if typologies are of much value, except in very gross terms, when the number and significance of variables is so great. The method is rather to examine a variety of exchange systems as a technique for uncovering some of the principles by which they work and change. In this way the relationship between exchange principles and social and economic development may be elucidated.

But one form of exchange has a special place in the literature. This is the market system. Unfortunately, once again there are different conceptions as to what a market system connotes, which can be most confusing to the unwary reader. The economist's usage is specifically and clearly an abstraction which can be applied to empirical situations only approximately. L. M. Fraser writes:

> The word "market" need not detain us long. In economics it means, not a particular building or locality, but a state of affairs. There is a "market" in a commodity (i.e., a commodity class) when there are a number of buyers and sellers, and when the unit price offered and paid by each is affected by the decisions of all the others. The market is said to be "perfect" when each buyer has full knowledge, and the ability to use it, of what every seller is demanding, and each seller has full knowledge, and the ability to use it, of what every buyer is offering . . .
> Both the concept of a commodity class and the concept of a perfect market are essentially abstract and "functional" terms. An approximation to their realization is to be found in the financial world. . . . But outside this circumscribed area the conditions envisaged by the theory of pure competition are not to be found in all their purity.[8]

Where these conditions do not obtain, there are imperfect markets of various sorts. But even these are model-building abstractions obtained through the conceptual alteration of limited variables. At most they can be applied to small sectors of an economy, never to a real world economy as a total.

Another way of approaching the market is to see it as a system which produces self-regulating prices. While this has a closer empirical refer-

---

[7] Compare the approach of George Homans, "Social Behavior as Exchange," in *Sentiments and Activities* (New York: Free Press of Glencoe, Inc., 1962).

[8] L. M. Fraser, *Economic Thought and Language* (London: Adam and Charles Black, Ltd., 1937), pp. 131-33.

ent, it is merely a gross classificatory tool without the analytical sharpness of the model-building market concept. Further, when we have examined the descriptive material in later chapters, we shall see that there are many ways in which exchange systems can regulate themselves through exchange ratios (prices). It is necessary to add that the self-regulation is through the interaction of buyers and sellers who operate impersonally, that is without regard to factors such as those of kinship, prestige, status, emotion, or in any other way than as buyer and seller. But a purist would cavil at this conception even applied to our own society alone. To talk of some exchange systems as market systems and others as nonmarket systems is bound to raise objections of classificatory accuracy.

Paul Bohannan and George Dalton seem closer when they write of the applicability or inapplicability, as the case might be, of the "market principle" to those institutions which they are empirically examining as market places.[9] Market places are sites, with social, economic, cultural, political, and other referents, where buyers and sellers (or perhaps exchangers of other types) meet for the purpose of exchange. The degree to which they use market principles is highly variable, but it may be that market principles are seldom wholly absent. It is also common to find market principles applied in quite other institutional contexts.

If we follow this view, we can take it one step further. We can replace the classificatory approach with one which asks to what degree, and in what form, market principles operate in specific exchange situations and systems. But the so-called market principle is not just one principle, but a compendium of principles. What we shall be asking should be, what are the characteristics of exchange systems with respect to:

(1) the impersonality or otherwise of the interaction of buyers and sellers (this we will have to translate into more adequate sociological categories);

(2) the systematization of exchange values (that is, prices), so that we may see whether and how they affect one another;

(3) the degree to which buying and selling of specific goods and services are specialized functions;

(4) the range of goods and services for which buying and selling are conventionally valid;

(5) the degree to which exchange transactions enter into the stages of production from raw resources to consumable product or service;

(6) the degree and nature of competition in buying and selling;

[9] Paul Bohannan and George Dalton, *Markets in Africa* (Evanston, Ill.: Northwestern University Press, 1962), pp. 1-2.

(7) the degree to which buying and selling may be differentiated through the interposition of a medium of exchange (if there is no medium of exchange, barter is an act of *both* buying and selling on the part of each individual)?

All these variables are essential aspects of the market principle.

MONEY

A similar approach can be applied to the vexing question of the analysis of money. Here again, money can be used as a classificatory empirical referent, denoting a class of commodities or accounting values used in specific ways to facilitate an exchange system. Arguments then abound as to whether this or that commodity or accounting value falls within the definition of money, hence whether money can be found in a society, hence whether the society is monetary or not. There is clearly a difference between capitalism, where cash represents a commodity which is applicable over the whole range of material exchanges and many nonmaterial ones, and the economy of Melanesia where there is no such universally applicable medium of exchange.

The reason I used the phrase "commodity or *accounting value*" in the previous paragraph is that even in capitalist society the notion of money is not restricted to the commodity, cash. Credit is part of the money supply, and this can be an abstraction. And it is generally accepted that the *quantity* of money is the resultant of many forces including the velocity of its circulation. In other words, money is not a physical thing in essence. Like the market, it is a compendium of functions.

Analytical economics defines these functions, which, following L. M. Fraser,[10] are, over and above the common reference to pieces of cash:

(1) as a medium of exchange and/or store of value;
(2) purchasing power;
(3) liquid or short-term capital;
(4) liquid reserves in general;
(5) units of value.

As a matter of interest, all these functions are logically dependent upon the characteristic of liquidity, that is the relative ease with which a commodity (or entry in an account book) can be exchanged. Durability, transferability, acceptability over a wide range of transactions, ease of accounting (including division and addition), all affect liquidity.

[10] Fraser, *op. cit.*

As is implied in some of the functions listed previously, cash and accounts are not the only liquid items in capitalism: stocks and shares, mortgages, grain futures, real property, are all liquid to some degree, and under some circumstances take on the functions of money. In primitive societies, which I am prepared to call nonmonetary, articles with maximum liquidity are usually lacking. That is, even those articles sometimes called "primitive money" are not exchangeable over the whole range of transactions.

Nevertheless, many monetary functions are present in commodities which at first sight may seem surprising. Agricultural produce, for example, may have a wide range of acceptability and represent exchange liquidity to a high degree. It should be noted in passing that the most systematic treatment of the functions of money-like articles in primitive society confuses some of these issues. Paul Einzig [11] is clear in his definitions of money and holds that only those articles which meet all his criteria should be called money. Unfortunately, he continues to call articles money that clearly do not meet his criteria, often on little more justification than that some observer or traveler called them money. This leads to considerable inconsistency in the treatment, which could be avoided if we simply asked what commodities are liquid and in what manner and degree. And what is their role in systematizing exchanges? [12]

One aspect of the transformation of simple economies into complex, dynamic ones is the increase in the extent of the market, that is, an increase in the range and quantity of transactions to which market principles apply, and an intensification of those principles. To a large extent, this is linked with an increase in exchange liquidity which can be described as the monetization of the economy.

[11] Paul Einzig, *Primitive Money* (London: Eyre & Spottiswoode [Publishers], Ltd., 1949).

[12] Compare my treatment of primitive and modern money in *Changing Melanesia* (Melbourne: Oxford University Press, 1954); and in "Changes in Heirloom Jewellery in the Central Solomons," *Oceania,* **20,** No. 3 (1950), 169-84.

In this chapter we shall examine some examples of systems of exchange which are based upon gift-giving, either directly or through ceremonial, and upon the ethical imperatives of reciprocal obligations. While the two features may be somewhat separated, they come together in time and place in systems of barter.

A usual approach is to consider reciprocity to be further from contemporary methods of trading than ceremonial exchange, since the latter is frequently interpreted as containing within it elements of monetization. This I believe to be a mistake, and in order to reinforce the point that the systems coexist, I shall treat the classical examples of ceremonial first, and then examine their relationship to reciprocity and barter. We are not concerned here with postulating an evolutionary sequence, or in stating that historically one form led to another. In the modern world, this is beside the point. We are rather concerned with discovering what these systems can tell us about the nature of exchange and its social ramifications, as a means of understanding contemporary problems of development. It should not be forgotten that the Trobriand Islands, the location of the classical *kula,* are a part of New Guinea, one of the latest on the list of emerging nations. And it will be postulated that elements analogous to those contained within these systems are a small but significant part of developing economies. Although the focus is on gift exchange,

CHAPTER TWO

Gift Exchange and Reciprocity

reciprocity, and barter, it should not be implied that these methods cover all of exchange in any one society. Ceremonial exchange and haggling markets can exist side by side.

TRADE RINGS OF PAPUA

The Trobriands are a group of low-lying tropical islands off the southeastern coast of Papua, which is the southernmost of the two Australian-administered territories in New Guinea. The people were studied between 1915 and 1918 by Bronislaw Malinowski, who was quickly recognized as the dean of British anthropological fieldworkers, and who described their culture in a series of richly detailed and evocative monographs. The first of these, *Argonauts of the Western Pacific,*[1] analyzed the institution of the *kula*, a ceremonial trade ring, which became a classical institution for anthropological discussion. It should be noted in passing that in 1964 the ceremonially oriented Trobrianders participated with the rest of the peoples of New Guinea in the first election by universal suffrage of representatives to the Legislative Council.

The central feature of the *kula* is the large expedition of sailing canoes which travels with great coordination and ritual preparation between Sinaketa in the Trobriands and Dobu to the south. The primary object is to facilitate the ceremonial exchange of prized ornaments. Malinowski referred primarily to the events surrounding this expedition, but he and Reo Fortune noted also the expeditions of the Dobuans who visited not only the Trobriands but the other islands to the south, including Tubetube. The people of Tubetube in turn linked with yet others to the northwest, such as Woodlark and Misima, and the people of Woodlark voyaged to the Marshall Bennett islands, whose villagers in turn linked up once again with the Trobriands to the east. Thus the voyages and the ceremonial exchanges constituted a complete circle, although there was a considerable variety of circumferential routes along which movement could be traced.

The objects which are ceremonially exchanged are collectively known as *vaygu'a*, and fall into two classes. One, *soulava*, consists of long necklaces of small discs ground and drilled from the spondylus shell. The other consists of polished white arm-shells, *mwali*.

To enter the *kula* ring a man must have knowledge of the appropriate etiquette and the magic which accompanies every stage of the pro-

---

[1] Bronislaw Malinowski, *Argonauts of the Western Pacific* (London: Routledge & Kegan Paul, Ltd., 1932).

ceedings and which ensures success, and he must have at least one ornament. Knowledge of etiquette is attained through general socialization, but much of the magic is idiosyncratic and must be learned specifically. A young man may obtain magical lore and his initial ornaments from either his father or his mother's brother, to whom he makes solicitory gifts. He then chooses a partner either from someone with whom his father already exchanged, or from someone else of his own choosing (Malinowski is vague on the latter point). The partnership is clinched by the presentation of the ornament as an opening gift.

The man who accepts the opening gift thereby promises to make a return gift of equivalent status but from the opposite class of objects. He may not be able to do this in the next visiting season, but he must nevertheless show he honors the promise by making some token gift, which itself must be reciprocated. Thus there may be several intermediary transactions before the exchange mechanism runs its course. The exchanges are accompanied by forms of words and ceremonial acts all of which reinforce the notions of honorable gift-giving and mutual dependence between persons who, in most instances, would be strangers in other circumstances. But since the institution has been passed on from generation to generation, so too has been the interlinkage of partners, a relationship which is itself passed on and developed through the generations.

The ceremonial nature of the *vaygu'a* is attested by the track of their movement. *Soulava* are always given to the person who, geographically speaking, lives in a clockwise direction from the donor; similarly *mwali* move counterclockwise. The objects may be worn, or rather displayed, through use as personal adornment on ritually important occasions, but their main significance is as a store of ceremonial wealth. A man who can accumulate them uses them to further extend his partnerships both in number and in velocity of circulation. As the objects move around the ring they come back eventually and pass through their geographical area of origin (though very seldom through their original owner's hands). Thus the village of Sinaketa manufactures *soulava* and sends them westward: it sends *mwali* south and actually receives *soulava* in return. Thus it "pays" for objects which it manufactures with objects it has to import.

The ring is not a single track. Each participant has a number of partners, the number depending upon his initiative and status, the latter being largely a reflection of his inherited and achieved ability to command the requisite supply of *vaygu'a*. The number of permutations and combinations of paths is thus mathematically very great indeed (A is partnered with B, C, D, each of whom is partnered with B_1, B_2, B_3, C_{1-4},

D_{1-5}, each of whom again is partnered with a number of others, and so on). Since the presentation of *vaygu'a* in the *kula* is a highly cere-monialized event, and since outside the *kula vaygu'a* are given in presentation on the most honorific occasions, particular valuables come to be associated with particular events, and thus accumulate a history. An ornament with a powerful history comes to be renowned and eagerly sought after; a person seeking it will make special presentations to his partner to influence him to part with it.

A man may visit his *kula* partner alone and privately, and frequently does this as between, for example, the easily accessible villages of the same island. But voyages between the Trobriands and other island groups involve canoes which require crews to man them, and the argonauts must run the gauntlet of potentially hostile weather, and of fantastic and vicious spiritual beings who inhabit the intervening reaches, and they must conduct their operations with partners living in communities of different culture, not bound by the same rules of overall behavior, nor answerable to a single political authority. For these dangers, group expeditions with powerful leadership (secular and ritual) and cooperative support provide effective security.

But when the representatives of one cultural-political entity visit others in large numbers, the potential hostility which could break out into active aggression must be reduced, compensated for, and controlled. This is partly achieved through the meticulous observance of a complex sequence of gift-giving between the representatives of the groups concerned, and partly by large-scale feasting and exchange of food.

Food exchange has a special place in the Trobriand economy. Any brief summary must do violence to a number of significant features, but I shall select for comment those which are most pertinent to our present theme. The first point to note is that agricultural food production is at the same time the most universally distributed skilled activity in the community and the one most basic to survival and prosperity. The man, or the family, which has produced most food in a season is most favored by the supernatural powers, has shown greatest prowess in the necessary skills, has placed himself in the position of maintaining his social obligations to the greatest extent, and has in all ways demonstrated his superiority according to the values of the people.

To grow and accumulate agricultural food, then, is the measure of a man's success and the road to the improvement of his prestige and status. But the food must be seen, known, and admired. Whenever a large group ceremony takes place, as with death or mourning, or at the time of harvest, the gardeners of the Trobriands vie with one another to heap for admiration the greatest piles of food, and to distribute these to relatives and persons whom they wish to honor. The display and distribution is what we call a "feast," but it should be noted that a feast is not a gluttonous or orgiastic event. The food, when distributed, is cooked and eaten in the home of the recipient.

Social structure in the Trobriands is based upon matrilineages, that is, descent groups in which children accede to membership in the lineage of the mother but not the father. The vertical division of society into lineages has an inherent tendency to fission, particularly when marriage and property are confined within the lineage, unless there is a strong political authority which resists the tendency of society to fly apart. In the Trobriands there is no such central political authority, but as in most lineal societies, the tendency towards fission is counterbalanced by the rule of exogamy and the obligations that go with it.

As we have seen, the children belong to the lineal group of their mother, which cannot be that of their father. Thus in any family, which is the basic unit of upbringing and production, two lineages join. Repeat this for all families, and the society is bound together through family responsibility. Further, mother and mother's brother belong to the same lineage, and mother's brother exercises considerable responsibility for the children. This is shown in many ways, but the most pertinent here is through what is known as the *urigubu* principle, which may be explained as follows.

Trobriand agriculture is highly diversified. There are ordinary food crops, and there is a ceremonial food which is a particular kind of yam. It is this yam which figures primarily in food display and distribution. In the institution of *urigubu* a mother's brother, at time of harvest, presents the bulk of his ceremonial yams to his sister's husband. Malinowski interprets this as showing the concern of the mother's brother for the well-being of the children, a gift from the real household head (mother's brother) to the family guardian (father). This interpretation he supports by a tenuous and far-fetched argument based upon presumed notions about the physiology of paternity in Trobriand society, which has been hotly debated in the literature.

A more satisfactory interpretation, in accord with what is known about other matrilineal societies, would hold that the gift, and the smaller returned acknowledgments, are of symbolic value indicating the mutual dependence of the two lineages, demonstrating that their association is fundamental and enduring. As Dorothy Lee has pointed out,[2] the mother's brother does not give altruistically, for the ceremonial yams *are not prized as food*. If he were giving altruistically (as he often

[2] Dorothy Lee, *Freedom and Culture* (Englewood Cliffs, N.J.: Prentice-Hall, Inc., 1959).

does in ordinary day-to-day relations) he would give other foods, including taro and bananas, which are used much more in domestic consumption. The gifts are symbolic, not a contribution to the nutritional budget. Following their receipt, the father will distribute many of them further by giving them to other persons within his lineage, thus indicating to the members of his corporate group that the relationship between the lineages is still of basic importance. Men with plural marriages in this polygynous society will be receiving *urigubu* from a variety of lineages. This clearly raises their status, increases the flow of ceremonial wealth into the lineage, and reinforces power through lineal alliance.

Other aspects of exchange are of considerable importance in the Trobriand economy, but unfortunately Malinowski was less concerned with delineating a model of the total economy than with analyzing the specific institutions mentioned previously. However, from passing references and short paragraphs we can glean some of the principles. One is that there was considerable day-to-day cooperation within families and between families linked through the lineage of their heads and between families linked through marriage. Such cooperation was naturally stronger when there was residential and land-owning propinquity.

Another is that there was a degree of specialization of skill, particularly in manufacture and in ritual leadership. Certain persons were skilled in aspects of canoe construction. Certain villages specialized in the manufacture of items such as *vaygu'a*, pottery, greenstone blades, and the like. Thus, there was exchange of services based upon division of labor, reciprocity, and mutual dependence, and in addition there was a need for trade in material things.

The *kula* itself was not oriented to individual trade in its ceremonial activities. But alongside the *kula* persons visiting their partners took advantage of the opportunity to engage in trade. Malinowski makes the point that *kula* partners would exchange gifts of a trade character in addition to *vaygu'a*, and that the security afforded by the partnership would make it possible for the visitor to make contact with other persons in the village and trade with them. This latter trade included a greater element of bargaining and less attention to the niceties of honorable gift-giving.

This leads to the question of the formation of exchange ratios, or prices. Dorothy Lee's examination of the material leads her to accept the position that there are differences in the valuation of different *vaygu'a*, depending upon their historical and symbolic role. But these differences are relatively static and are sharply to be distinguished from valuation arrived at through barter haggling. Malinowski himself leans to this view on occasion, as when he sharply distinguishes trade from the *kula*. In part this is a confusion arising from a relative lack of data on the details of trading exchange, but even more it comes from a lack of theoretical consistency on Malinowski's part, as Raymond Firth pointed out in his discussion of Malinowski's approach to valuation.[3] Malinowski's material on the *kula* is quite explicit. A single *kula* exchange consists of a series of gifts, of which at least one is a supplicatory gift designed to influence the owner of a *vaygu'a* to part with it. There is no set, uniform, or standardized exchange ratio which explicitly relates differences in value associated with differences in quality of the *vaygu'a*. These matters are regulated through the judgment of the partners as to whether the ornaments exchanged are indeed appropriately equivalent, and any hesitancy is dealt with through the intermediary exchanges or by prolonging the exchanges until both partners are satisfied. This is not the rough haggling of the bazaar. But it certainly is delicately negotiated price adjustment of the same kind. The difference is not in the principles of valuation, but in the etiquette of negotiation.

There has also been discussion as to whether the valuables constitute money. Both Malinowski and M. J. Herskovits[4] following him held that the valuables were not money in any acceptable sense. Malinowski argued that there could not be money since there were no prices; this we have seen to be wrong, since all exchange ratios were negotiated and hence prices emerged. But he also said that there was no established mechanism of exchange. This indicates in a vague way that the criterion we adopted earlier is not satisfied, that is, neither the valuables nor any other commodity serves to induce a system of interconnectedness throughout the exchange transactions.

Yet Einzig[5] criticizes this approach. He admits that there is no single medium of exchange, but asks why should we not recognize *several* currencies (namely *vaygu'a,* yams, and nowadays, trade tobacco), each with a limited use. However, this leads to the position that anything which is given up in order to obtain anything else is money, and one might then say that anything exchanged is money.

So we are back in the position outlined in Chapter One, namely that the real question is what degree of liquidity is shown by the various objects which enter into exchange? The answer for the Trobriands is that the liquidity of *vaygu'a* is severely limited by their high degree of value: they cannot be used in transactions of low value. Other manufactured

---

[3] Raymond Firth, ed., *Man and Culture* (London: Routledge & Kegan Paul, Ltd., 1957), pp. 219-21.

[4] M. J. Herskovits, *Economic Anthropology* (New York: Alfred A. Knopf, Inc., 1952), Chap. XI.

[5] Paul Einzig, *Primitive Money* (London: Eyre & Spottiswoode [Publishers], Ltd., 1949), p. 83.

objects are limited by high value (as with canoes) or low velocity of circulation. Of all traditional items, yams have perhaps the greatest liquidity. They are widely acceptable in transactions and can be combined for high or low values. Their liquidity is limited by the relatively short durability (one year to eighteen months at the very most), which makes it impossible to store them for future transactions beyond a certain period.

Dorothy Lee, drawing heavily upon Malinowski's data and interpretations, presents a convincing argument [6] to the effect that Trobriand society is stable, patterned, and unchanging, and that this orientation is rooted in the philosophy and conceptualization of the people. She shows, for example, that the history of the *vaygu'a* is less a matter of their development of value than an ingredient of their being, an essential part of their given quality. Giving is good in itself; it is not carried out in order to achieve other purposes. The validity and goodness of one's existence is not in one's achievement but in being part of the pattern of culture and society, "as a fixed point in a single, changeless whole." The *urigubu* gift is not for achievement or altruism, but is worthy in itself, as part of the act of role fulfillment, which in turn is part of the total pattern. Gift-giving escapes the purposiveness of barter, which is despised. The pattern is satisfying to the individual, since everything is known and securely predictable.

Now there is much to be said for this point of view as an interpretation of the philosophy of the Trobrianders, but as a model of the workings of Trobriand economy and society it is too remote from the realities. Anthropologists have been slow in recognizing this, since many of Malinowski's generalizations are in accord with this interpretation. Yet other Melanesian societies are so clearly competitive and dynamic that the only solution seemed to be to regard the Trobriands as somehow aberrant.

Fortunately another solution has been proposed by J. P. Singh Uberoi [7] which is equally in accord with the Malinowski data, is more consistent with more recent studies of other Melanesian societies, and seems closer to reality. Uberoi bases his analysis upon a close examination of the dynamic principles inherent in the social structure and the way in which the exchanges influence a person's position in it. The model which emerges is one of dynamic competition for sociopolitical status based upon the use of wealth to control social relationships.

[6] Lee, *op. cit.*

[7] J. P. Singh Uberoi, *Politics of the Kula Ring* (Manchester: Manchester University Press, 1962).

The exchange of gifts creates or reinforces relationships of alliance between individuals and the groups of which they are representative. They open the way for the exchange of other acts of duty and support, both material and nonmaterial. In the *kula* ring, the partnership establishes an alliance with political overtones, in that law and order is guaranteed between the communities involved. It opens channels of substantial trade and social intercourse. But a man's position in the ring is not predetermined and static. A participant starts from a position of relative capital advantage or disadvantage, capital here including his actual stock of *vaygu'a* and his indirect control of them through his effective relationships with other persons, and hence his ability to call upon their stocks. From this position, if he is ambitious, he may maneuver to increase the number and scale of alliances, and hence his command over the flow of wealth and the degree to which his good will is sought, and hence his status and prestige.

Malinowski made much of the position of certain chiefs as if they occupied their position solely through ascriptive status. Uberoi has shown from Malinowski's data that they were rather *primus inter pares*, holding their position, achieving it, or letting it slip, according to their ability to maneuver the social and ceremonial relationships, including those of both *kula* and *urigubu*. This is much more in accord with general Melanesian operations, and gives a motivation for success in the exchanges.

Rivalry shows itself in other ways. Marriage is a form of alliance legitimated by the continuance of *urigubu;* there is competition to excel in the *urigubu* presentations, and a motive to extend the number of wives through polygynous marriage, and hence the flow of goods and ceremonial recognition. At harvest time, or on the occasion of a quarrel, men prove their worth aggressively and competitively through the display of garden produce. This is no quiet statically patterned society in which every man has a fixed place. It is one in which a man stands or falls by his achievements, which can be summarized as his ability to establish the social relationships which contribute to his status.

It may be asked, if the Trobrianders were truly competitive in outlook and accumulation-oriented, why was the Trobriand economy, taken as a whole, not growing? An answer to such a question can only be speculative, but a number of factors do stand out. For example, the *range* of material things that the culture requires is severely limited. And with the exception of display food and *vaygu'a*, the quantities required to meet consumption needs are relatively small. There is not much point, for example, in accumulating a vast number of baskets or houses, and even the number of trading canoes that can be used is limited. Thus there can be no question of relating production to an infinitely expanding schedule of wants.

As far as food and *vaygu'a* are concerned, the position is a little different. While nutritional consumption of food may have a peak (and we do not know whether in traditional society it reached that peak), theoretically there would be no limit to the quantities of food used in display, since it could be (and sometimes is) left to rot. But since food can be stored for only a finite period of time, the quantity available at any point cannot exceed by much the productive capacity of the people in any one season, and this in turn is severely restricted, not by the environment, but by a static technology. Dynamic growth cannot be expected here.

Vaygu'a on the other hand are durable. It should be noted that in fact we do not have statistics showing whether their stock has increased over the years. Such an increase, with inflation of ceremonial, has been demonstrated for other societies in Melanesia in modern times.[8] But the effects of such an increase, should it occur, are confined to the range of transactions for which *vaygu'a* are appropriate, that is to ceremonial transactions. The result of an increase in supply could be either an extension of the ramifications of ceremonial, that is in its complexity, or in an inflation of particular transactions. It is quite possible, though not demonstrable, that the very complexity of the *kula* is in major part a function of the available quantity of valued ornaments. This might have had some effect on the total Trobriand economy, since it might have led to extensions of partnerships into new areas and an increase in peripheral trade.

THE KWAKIUTL POTLATCH

The word potlatch in North American English has come to refer variously to feasting or to trading, with an implication of giveaway prices in the latter case. But in technical anthropology it refers to a complex institution of ceremonial wealth accumulation and dispersal found, with variations, among the coastal cultural groups of northwestern North America. I shall concentrate upon the analysis of the potlatch of the Kwakiutl, who inhabit the northern part of Vancouver Island and adjacent islands and settlements near the mainland of British Columbia.

The potlatch, like the *kula,* is a subject of classical discussion. The primary reason for this is the attention drawn to it by the pioneering

[8] See, for example, Cyril S. Belshaw, *The Great Village* (London: Routledge & Kegan Paul, Ltd., 1957).

ethnographer, Franz Boas, who produced one of the earliest and most voluminous accounts of any culture. The primary reference to the potlatch is in his monograph "The Social Organization and the Secret Societies of the Kwakiutl Indians," [9] but other pertinent references abound throughout his writing. Unfortunately, even more than Malinowski, Boas was writing at a time before major theoretical advances had been made, and he was by temperament more interested in getting out the record than in theoretical construction. The result is that his data are often not explicit enough for settling theoretical issues, despite its volume, and much reinterpretation is necessary. Another major reference, which brings together much of the historical material, is Helen Codere's monograph, *Fighting with Property*.[10]

The potlatch was attacked by the Canadian authorities as being wasteful and destructive of moral and economic initiative, in other words as standing in the way of development and modernization. Although it continued for some time illegally, the potlatch died in its old form, mainly as a result of repression. This was despite the fact that during its illegal continuance into the twenties, the Kwakiutl came to terms with the alien economic system, and some became substantial commercial fishing entrepreneurs. After the Depression, both the potlach and Kwakiutl commercial initiative suffered setbacks. Winter ceremonial dances, associated to a considerable degree with potlatching, still continue with regenerative vigor among the more urbanized Salish peoples of southern British Columbia and northern Washington.

The basic unit of corporate action in Kwakiutl society is called the *numaym*. There is so much confusion in the accounts of Boas and in the subsequent interpretations that it would take a major study to provide a definitive account of the composition and functions of the *numaym*. In one passage,[11] for which G. P. Murdock [12] severely takes him to task, Boas holds that the *numaym* represents a confusion of matrilineal and patrilineal elements resulting from hypothetical historical pressures. From time to time he implies that the *numaym* is a bilateral group, but the implications of descent, inheritance, acquisition of title, access to property, corporate action, and marriage rules are not clearly distinguished in

[9] Franz Boas, "The Social Organization and the Secret Societies of the Kwakiutl Indians," in *Annual Report of the Smithsonian Institution for 1895* (Washington, D.C.: Government Printing Office, 1897).

[10] Helen Codere, *Fighting with Property*, Monograph XVIII of the American Ethnological Society (New York: J. J. Augustin, Inc.—Publisher, 1950).

[11] Boas, "The Social Organization and the Secret Societies of the Kwakiutl Indians," p. 334.

[12] G. P. Murdock, *Social Structure* (New York: The Macmillan Company, 1949), pp. 190-91.

analysis, so that we must go back to the data to find out in what sense the "group" is a group. This confusion seems to affect Murdock as well, since on page 190 of *Social Structure* he says "the Kwakiutl are essentially bilateral in their social structure," but in a table on page 230 he lists traits which are largely patrilineal, and on the all-important matter of descent refers to "patrilineal descent without exogamous kin groups." Boas in his later analysis [13] decided to abandon such classification and simply regarded the *numaym* as unique, to be referred to as a *numaym* and nothing else. H. G. Barnett says equally bluntly that the *numaym* is patrilineal.[14]

We cannot avoid the issue completely, since some conception of the workings of the *numaym* is essential to any interpretation of the potlatch and its surrounding socioeconomic system. My interpretation runs as follows.

The *numaym* is essentially a patrilineal descent group with several well-defined corporate functions. These include maintenance of order within the group, the administration of land and sea resources owned by it, and the regulation of marriage and relations with other similarly organized groups. The corporate nature of the *numaym* is strengthened by its characteristic of patrilocal community residence and its ability to act together for joint production.

Within the *numaym* there is a complex system of titles which indicate a man's position and prerogatives. The primary acquisition of a title is by inheritance through primogeniture. Thus the eldest child in a family holds the inherited title, is regarded as the symbolic, ceremonial, and political representative of the family and administrator of its joint property. The senior title holder among the families who make up the *numaym* is similarly the ceremonial and political representative of the *numaym* and the administrator of the corporate property.

As with all patrilineal descent groups of complexity, the validation of patrilineality is in some respects fictional. With the Kwakiutl it is possible to show, through genealogy and mythology, that through time *numaym* accepted into their membership persons from other descent groups by immigration or by stressing the connection through their mothers. Such flexible mechanisms do not destroy the principle of patrilineality.

But in addition to acquiring titles through patrilineal inheritance, persons may acquire them by other methods, and it is this possibility which leads to the essential flexibility, and competitiveness, of the Kwakiutl social system, and the confusion in the analysis. All acquisition of title,

[13] Franz Boas, "The Social Organization of the Kwakiutl," *American Anthropologist,* **22** (1920), 111-26.

[14] H. G. Barnett, "The Nature of the Potlatch," *American Anthropologist,* **40** (1938), 349-58.

whether patrilineal or not, must be validated through potlatch. Conversely, one may acquire title through one's wife which may be passed on to one's children, each step requiring potlatch. There is some indication that patrilineally inherited titles and other titles are distinguished from each other, but there is no doubt that both contribute to a man's prestige and standing. It thus pays to manipulate marriage ties, which can be done flexibly through polygyny. Boas and Codere both refer to a surplus of titles in the society, since with depopulation not all could be assigned or validated. It is probable that this was a continuous feature of the system, however, since a surplus of titles would contribute to a rapidity of circulation or ceremonial exchange among them.

Boas implies throughout his writing, without saying so directly, that acquisition of a title implies membership in the *numaym* to which the title belongs. Thus, if one obtains a title through one's mother or wife, one becomes a member of her *numaym*. What constitutes membership is never specifically defined in this context. My own interpretation is that the acquisition of a title in this way does not necessarily imply corporate privileges in the associated *numaym*. It does however symbolically affirm a link between the two *numaym*, which is an important demonstration of social power. Further, it implies that the affinal *numaym* is in fact giving some of its property away along the lines of marriage links, for a title is in every respect to be regarded as a piece of incorporeal property. It may even be divided or shared by several individuals.

If a title is seen to be, in essence, property and indeed as an element in wealth, its transfer and exchange can be much more readily understood than if it is thought to represent solely a social role. Further, as with the *kula*, the exchanges can be seen as validating or symbolizing social relationships between groups linked by marriage. With the Kwakiutl as with the Trobrianders there is a principle of lineal descent. Exogamous marriage welds together different lineages, cemented by rivalrous ceremonial exchange, which indicates both difference and solidarity.

There are two modifications to this model for the Kwakiutl. One is that for various reasons (death of his father, disagreement with siblings, lack of resources) a person may wish to leave his *numaym*. The one to which he would naturally turn for support would be his mother's, and entry would be easier if he had a title derived from that *numaym*. This may account for the bilateral confusion. The second is that Boas refers to endogamous marriages carried out to keep property within the *numaym* and reducing the temptation to give it away affinally.[15] This point may be the basis of Murdock's reference to lack of exogamous kin groups. But in the same passage Boas states that this is most exceptional.

15 Boas, "The Social Organization of the Kwakiutl," p. 117.

(His statement is ambiguous in that there may be only *one* case recorded in his genealogies, or only *very few*.) Such exceptional endogamy can be found in many other societies without invalidating the general principle of exogamy and the system on which it is based. Perhaps it might be true for the Kwakiutl that a growth in the fanatical pursuit of wealth (which can be demonstrated) might eventually have led to a breakdown in affinal linkage and an emphasis on endogamy, but this is pure speculation.

Although there are scattered references in the writings of eighteenth-century seamen to matters peripheral to the potlatch, direct recorded observation of the institution occurred only in the nineteenth century when the articles which entered into it had already been influenced by Western trading and pressure. These articles had apparently included slaves, but the nineteenth-century list emphasized Hudson's Bay Company blankets, canoes, food, miscellaneous manufactured articles, and the all-important copper. This last was a shield-like sheet of copper, often decorated with indented design. It constituted a peak of value in the potlatch, although its inherent cash value was slight. Among these articles, the blankets were the most common and they were the unit of account, the potlatch value of all other articles being convertible into them, and all other articles being exchangeable for them. Thus they did in fact represent a wide and flexible medium of exchange.

As in most other direct exchange systems, a man could become a creditor by making a gift which could not be refused and which would have to be returned on demand. In any such system a man may build up substantial credit by this means and call it in at a time of major need. By this means, his wealth has been used in the meantime, has been preserved, and has reinforced the all-important social links. Among the Kwakiutl, a dynamic is introduced through a system of extreme interest payments, reflected in the following table:

Kwakiutl Interest Rates *

Term	Number blankets borrowed	Return demanded	Rate
Under six months	5	6	20%
Six months	5	7	40%
Twelve months	5	10	100%
Twelve months when borrower has poor credit	5	17	233%

* Helen Codere, *Fighting with Property*, p. 70, after Boas.

This made it possible for a man to enter a potlatch in a very short space of time, or to build up the quantity of goods involved to a fantastic peak. A young man, for example, borrows, let us say, one hundred blankets from ranking persons in the *numaym* of the tribal subdivision of the Kwakiutl to which his own *numaym* belonged. He lends these to other persons, who, knowing of his plans to enter the potlatch, repay them in a month at the 100 per cent rate of interest plus an additional premium of 100 per cent. He now has control over 300 blankets. He then makes a further loan, repaid in the same manner, and further added to by outright gifts from such close kinsmen as his father.

By these methods, at the end of one year he is likely to have control of over 400 blankets. This quantity is sufficient for him to engage in a formal potlatch, though of minor quantity. He can repay most of his loans during the potlatch and with a small surplus make the essential potlatch gifts to *numaym* other than his own.[16]

One difficulty of interpretation is that Boas did not trace through actual cases of accumulation and distribution with detailed reference to sources, and his generalized accounts differ. The support in the potlatching group is sometimes referred to as the tribe, sometimes as the *numaym*, and the literature frequently states that in a potlatch the *numaym* or the tribe is on its honor to support the potlatcher, and the potlatch must be distributed to *numaym* other than his own. One suspects that, as with Melanesian analogues, the supporting social unit depends on the ability and status of the potlatcher, and particularly his skill in distributing the original gifts to create the appropriate indebtedness. This may be done within his own group, since it is relatively informal, and is for the purposes of engendering support.

The formal potlatch, however, involves vast and complex ceremonial, all designed to emphasize a kind of love-hate relationship with some other social group. This clearly cannot be one's own *numaym*, and if one has high status within one's tribe, it could not be one's tribe. Both the literature and the logic of such societies indicate the high probability that most potlatches will be held on occasions for the emphasis of the rivalrous solidarity of affinally connected groups. This is consistent with the following potlatch occasions: marriage, the first-birth of a child, the initiation of one's sister's son into a secret society, the validation of the succession of one's own son by potlatching to affinal groups who might claim him for their own. Indeed, the Tlingit neighbors of the Kwakiutl make mortuary ceremonies the prime occasion of potlatching. Mortuary ceremonies are classically occasions for affinal cooperation,

---

[16] Franz Boas, "The Social Organization and Secret Societies of the Kwakiutl Indians," p. 341, modified by Codere in *Fighting with Property,* p. 72.

if for no other reason than to demonstrate the mother's claim to her child, and some theorists have seen the mortuary implications as a driving force in potlatch.[17]

On each of these occasions the groups taking responsibility perform services for their affinally linked connections. The solidarity thus demonstrated is tempered by an attempt to do more than the linked groups could reciprocate, that is, to show superiority by rivalrous competition in performing the obligations.

A more persistent theme in the potlatch is the validation of social position, symbolized in the acquisition and holding of a title and improving its status. As with the *urigubu* distributions of the Trobriands, status competition and distribution competition go hand in hand. But with the Kwakiutl, competition is a much more frenetic and inflated affair. As with the Trobriands, it contains the component of challenging one's rival to do better, and thus stimulates production and accumulation. But it also includes a strong element of denigration, or deriding the other fellow, and this carries over into a show of contemptuous and arrogant hostility. In the Trobriands, to give too much would be a cause for envy, bitterness, and recrimination, and great care is taken to avoid this. Among the Kwakiutl, to give too much is the whole point of the game. The greatest potlatchers of all are those who not only give fantastic amounts, making it well-nigh impossible for their rivals to repay in a future potlatch at the appropriate interest, but who also demonstrate how rich and magnificent they are by actually destroying their most valued items: canoes, coppers, blankets, even stocks of fish grease and oil. The destruction of property is the most dramatic and characteristic feature of the potlatch.

The culmination of the greatest potlatch was the destruction of the highest embodiment of value, namely the copper, an act which would redound to the fame and status of the potlatcher for all time. But Helen Codere has drawn attention to another feature of copper destruction, namely that it destroyed the value accumulated and embodied in it. I would add the point that with interest rates as high as they were, some such feature was essential to the maintenance of the system, for no imaginable increase in supply, and no imaginable increase in velocity of circulation, could possibly permit the continuance of transactions at 100 per cent interest ad infinitum. In order to obtain a copper, a man had to accumulate considerable equivalent value; the destruction of the copper removed that value from circulation and hence acted as a brake upon inflation.

[17] Cf. Philip Drucker, "Rank, Wealth and Kinship in Northwest Coast Society," *American Anthropologist,* **41** (1939), 55-70.

At the same time, the coppers did not disappear entirely, and could enter circulation once again to attract value to them. The destruction was physical—breaking into pieces or melting on a fire—but the material was still usually retained. Broken pieces of coppers themselves continued to circulate, but they could be re-bolted together. Unfortunately we do not know what the effect of re-bolting would be on value by comparison with the initial unbroken state. Melted coppers could be re-formed by smiths. Furthermore, of course, material could be obtained from traders at fractional value.

In the discussion of the *kula* I speculated that inflation might have led to an elaboration of ceremonial. We can be a little more positive on this issue for the potlatch: indeed I would argue that the potlatch as we know it for the nineteenth century was almost entirely a result of inflation.

However, the standard theory of the potlatch is that it is a result of the great indigenous wealth of the Kwakiutl.[18] The natural environment, so the argument runs, provided a plentiful supply of all kinds of fish, game, and wild vegetable food, so that with a minimal expenditure of energy the people could accumulate vast surplus resources.

This, to say the least, is a dubious argument, which reminds one of the myth of idyllic life on South Sea atolls. It has never been substantiated by careful economic analysis. In particular, it ignores the element that the major scarce resource was human labor: however plentiful the biological supplies, the resources could be converted to use only through human labor, which placed specific limits on accumulation. Against this, most important food resources in the area could be preserved for long periods of time (much more so than in tropical climates). But even here, one has to bear in mind that food supplies had to maintain populations over long periods of seasonal shortage, and through the winter months when activities had to be directed toward indoor interests.

The natural environment and traditional technology of the Kwakiutl was certainly sufficient to provide a basis for a potlatch economy in its essentials, but it is at least doubtful whether it would provide for the regular and dramatically large destruction of property except in times of windfall. The potlatch as we know it from direct observation seems rather to have been the result of modern influences injecting quantitative forces into the traditional institution, spinning it into whirling inflation and competitive vortex. The two major forces, which Helen Codere has clearly set out, were depopulation and the entry of monetary trading

[18] See, for example, Irving Goldman in Margaret Mead, ed., *Cooperation and Competition among Primitive Peoples* (New York: McGraw-Hill Book Company, 1937); and Helen Codere, *Fighting with Property*, p. 63.

into the economy. In addition, as a stabilizing factor, coppers were introduced, *apparently for the first time.*

Early population estimates are subject to a wide variety of errors, and the speculation of John Work that the 1836 population was over 23,000 was certainly too high. Another estimate for 1853 giving a figure of 7,000 is probably much nearer the mark. Official figures, which began for 1872 with a figure of 3,500 are probably on the low side. The trend, however, is consistent and in one direction during the nineteenth century, with a figure of 1,889 for 1884 and 1,345 for 1903, with numerous reports of ravaging and fatal epidemics. One of Helen Codere's objections to the early high estimates is that they would indicate a 90 per cent decline in less than fifty years. This however is precisely the rate of decline which is demonstrable for small Oceanic populations hit by similar scourges at the same period of history.

Whatever the rate might have been, the potlatch result was certain. With remarkable vitality, the Kwakiutl did not fall to pieces, but retained the vigor of their ceremony. But now titles were in great supply, chasing, as it were, fewer and fewer people. It was possible and practicable for younger scions of families to enter the potlatch, whereas once it may have been difficult. The quantity of durable goods per capita must have increased, and the effect on the productive economy of destroying a canoe, for example, must have been much less significant. Population decline thus had an inflationary effect, although in time this might have evened off.

The entry of the Kwakiutl into commercial life was even more significant. Helen Codere provides figures from Indian Agents to show a total income in 1906, for a population of 1,257 of $80,985. Prior to this time, and certainly from the 1830's, such activities as hunting, trapping, and fishing led to a cash income. In these early days, a very high proportion of such income would be available for spending on the main potlatch goods, namely blankets and copper. A standard price for a Hudson's Bay blanket was fifty cents. A minimal hypothetical income of $2,000 for the whole community in the early century sounds small, but it could be responsible for the annual addition of two thousand blankets into a fast declining population, and still leave $1,000 for other purposes. This is a very marked change from a situation in which a traditional blanket would have to be manufactured by time-consuming and laborious processes.

In the late nineteenth century, with income much higher, demand for generally manufactured wants would also be greater, but the opportunity to introduce the blankets could nevertheless have been of phenomenal proportions. This is borne out by Helen Codere's figures of actual potlatches. In 1849 there was a potlatch which included 20 woolen and 240 traditional blankets. This is the last year in which the traditional blankets appear in the lists. In 1869 there was a potlatch of 9,000 blankets. From 1893, figures of 12,000, 18,000, and 14,500 occur, with a culmination in 1936 of 33,000. While there is much doubt about the reliability of the figures in detail, inflation there certainly was in the second half of the nineteenth century and the first of the twentieth.

The history of the use of coppers is not so well documented. The accepted theory has been that in the eighteenth century the northwest-coast peoples obtained native copper ore and manufactured coppers themselves. But this was not based on a careful review of the evidence, and a recent exploratory study [19] has failed to find a single copper in European or American museums which is made of native copper. References to such coppers in the writings of seamen, explorers, and others is based on hearsay and can be shown to be of dubious authenticity. On the other hand, beginning in the eighteenth century, there was a lively trade in sheet copper. But it was not until 1804 that a European first saw a copper in potlatch form, and it was not until well into the late nineteenth century that references became frequent. It seems almost certain that coppers did not enter into the potlatch until trading in sheet copper began, and it is very likely that their use to destroy value and inhibit runaway inflation did not become clarified until the mid or late nineteenth century.

The Kwakiutl potlatch is a classical case of inflated social and ceremonial development consequent upon an improvement in wealth, coupled to the retention of traditional values.

EAST AFRICAN CATTLE COMPLEX

Many of the peoples of eastern and southeastern Africa are noted for the part played by cattle in their ceremonial exchange and ritual life. In some ways "cattle complex" is a misnomer, taking its cue as it does from the material role of cattle rather than from the structure of the institutions themselves. If we take the use of cattle rather than of some other commodities as the starting point, the complex appears very different from the potlatch or *kula* where cattle do not enter at all. But, after all, livestock in the form of pigs fulfill much the same role in many Melanesian societies, and even in cattle-complex societies in Africa goats and sheep can be of considerable parallel importance. If

[19] E. L. Keithahn, "Origin of the 'Chief's Copper' or Tinneh," unpublished paper read to the 13th Alaska Science Conference, 1962. I am indebted to Dr. H. B. Hawthorn for this reference. The careful study on which it is based is continuing.

we were to neutralize, as it were, the notion of cattle, and think rather of x, or ceremonial objects, and if we were to call potlatch or *kula* objects x as well, the emphasis in analyzing the cattle complex would be on social relationships which could be seen to have much affinity with both potlatch and *kula*.

One might, however, make further distinctions as to the nature and implications of the ceremonial objects. If x is the general class of ceremonial objects, x_1 can be thought of as those objects the use of which bears interest as an institutional arrangement, and x_2 those which contain within themselves reproductive elements as a fact of nature. Empirically, x is present in the Trobriands, x_1 in the potlatch and in other societies such as that of Rossel Island, and x_2 in the cattle complex, and other societies where livestock is used.

The societies of Africa are highly varied, but it is nevertheless possible to discern certain institutional themes which are of frequent occurrence. Some of these relate to a man's position in his descent group and with respect to its affinal linkages. Others relate to trading partnerships and friendships. And yet others relate to a man's position in his age set, which in Africa has important military, political, and ritual functions, and in some societies is highly organized. It is perhaps of some significance that age sets are not present in the same form in Melanesia or North America, but that there are other institutions which have similar implications for social structure. Among these are the societies of the North American Indians and the New Hebrides into which a man must be initiated through ritual exchanges involving ceremonial objects.

Age-set initiation in some ways brings out the nature of cattle exchange most clearly. Among the Pokot (Suk) of Kenya [20] the initiate obtains the ritual ox, not from his own herd, but by requesting it from a wealthy and influential man in return for the gift of a heifer. There then follows an elaborate ceremony of slaughter, the taking of omens, initiation into the status of adulthood, and food consumption, in which many male supporters are involved. According to J. G. Peristiany, this feast, *sapana*, "is the first step on the ladder of ceremonies which determine a man's age-status." Harold K. Schneider lists a series of "*sapana*-like feasts," most of which are concerned with some element of ritual cleanliness. But, as is common in such societies, ritual action involves social relations. It requires the support of one's fellows not merely in organizational terms, but as an indication that the principals concerned

---

[20] See J. G. Peristiany, "The Age-set System of the Pastoral Pokot," *Africa*, **21** (1951), 188-206; H. K. Schneider, "The Subsistence Role of Cattle among the Pokot and in East Africa," *American Anthropologist*, **59** (1957), 278-300.

are in harmony with their fellows. To be in harmony with one's fellows increases the likelihood that one is in harmony with spiritual forces, both in general, and in the particular sense that one may also be in harmony with a wide range of ancestral beings.

The act of exchanging a heifer for an ox carries with it wider significance. Whereas the steer is killed in the ceremony and consumed as meat (the fate of most steers), the heifer is preserved. Although the heifer must be fed and cared for, it carries the probability of reproduction. Depending on the society and the circumstances, the recipient may keep some of the progeny, but in all cases he acknowledges the act of the donor by continuing over the years to give him gifts. Such gifts may be the calves (or some of them) produced by the heifer, and other valuable articles. The occasion of gift-giving is usually when the donor visits the recipient, and it may be when one or other of the partners is in need of ritual or legal help.

This relationship is known among the Pokot as *tilia,* and is of major exchange significance. Peristiany points out that the initial *sapana* exchange establishes for the young initiate a life-long link with an influential person, who belongs to a lineage "with which intermarriages have been frequent as they have proved stable, fertile, and have resulted in long-lived offspring." It is not clear whether this is the lineage into which the young man ultimately marries, but affinal alliances are in some sense involved. Schneider shows that this and other *tilia* exchanges provide the basis for trading partnerships, and that, as with *kula* and potlatch, the crisscrossing of regularized relationships binds the society together. Elizabeth Colson,[21] writing of the Plateau Tonga of Northern Rhodesia, stresses the point that the gift exchanges establish an expectation of reciprocal behavior (which is a general characteristic of gift-giving) and that among the Tonga this has legal implications which indicate that rights in persons are thereby established. Further, these rights are in a sense shared by a collectivity, namely lineal kindred, who may require an individual to exercise them on their behalf (for example, when cattle are to be collected for a marriage exchange). Kinsfolk thus have an interest in supporting and maintaining the relationships, an interest which is the basis of legal action. And since cattle are passed from one generation to another, the rights that go with them are also inherited, and younger people have such a dominant interest in the administration of cattle held by older people that they may in fact seize cattle physically before death effects their inheritance.

The gift of cattle from groom's family to bride's is an essential element

[21] Elizabeth Colson, "The Role of the Cattle among the Plateau Tonga of Mazabuka District," *Rhodes-Livingstone Journal,* 11 (1951), 10-46.

in marriage ceremony and contract. This has often been interpreted as a contract between two individuals for the maintenance of a household. It is far less this than a means of establishing *tilia*-like social relationships between two kin groups now linked affinally. E. E. Evans-Pritchard has forcefully drawn attention to this aspect of bridewealth for the Nuer and the Azande.[22] For the former, the ideal payment at time of marriage is forty head of cattle, twenty for the bride's father's disposal, and twenty for the bride's mother's disposal. Out of each group of twenty, ten are held respectively by father and mother and their sons, as a family stock for subsequent circulation at the time of a future marriage. The remainder are distributed to the father's and mother's siblings and parents. Each of these distributory transactions is, as Evans-Pritchard puts it, "perhaps chiefly an acknowledgment of obligations between siblings and towards affines."

Evans-Pritchard is quite specific in his view that marriage payments are but one expression of the more general phenomenon of gift-giving as an indication of social relationships.

For marriage relations are not the only ones expressed in payments. The relations between chief and commoner, between father and son, between a lover and his sweetheart, to mention only three Zande examples, all employ techniques of gifts or payments which define the relations between the persons concerned and enable them to foresee the behavior of one another in given situations since the payments evoke the behavior. A full study of bridewealth must treat it as one of a number of techniques which employ wealth by gift or payment as a means of establishing, defining, expressing, and evoking social behavior.[23]

Furthermore, marriage establishes highly valued links between the respective kin groups. Levirate and sororate, Evans-Pritchard points out, maintain and reinforce these links.

In our examples from other areas, we have stressed the manipulability of such exchanges to gain personal social ends, such as status and authority. There is some debate as to how this applies within cattle-complex societies. Certainly some African societies are highly achievement-motivated. Political rivalry and expansion were notable characteristics of many Bantu groups, for example. But the link between wealth,

[22] E. E. Evans-Pritchard, "Nuer Bridewealth," *Africa,* **16** (1946), 247-57; and "Social Character of Bridewealth with Special Reference to the Azande," *Man,* **34** (1934), 172-75.

[23] Evans-Pritchard, "Social Character of Bridewealth with Special Reference to the Azande," p. 172.

status, and ambition in the better described cattle societies has not been clearly expressed. One recent scholar, Harold Schneider, even goes out of his way to play down the relationship. He writes,

> . . . cattle heroes are honored more for their prowess and cunning in raiding neighboring tribes for cattle than for their wealth, and community leaders seem to be singled out largely because of their knowledge and ability or for other such reasons. Still, cattle wealth is undeniably a source of prestige and some status.[24]

A man who (rarely) has 100 head of cattle is given deference but does not exercise political dominance.

But the analysis should not end there. Peristiany's view of Schneider's Pokot is that "the initiate begins his adult life by artificially enlarging his circle of potential protectors and friends," and his manipulation of *tilia* relationships enables him to carry this through life. He also holds that in distribution, contrary to the egalitarian theory of the Pokot, the rich in fact receive special attention. An outsider viewing Melanesian society would have some difficulty in identifying the rich authoritative men, since their riches are not clearly visible, and since their authority is expressed, not by an ability to give arbitrary orders, but through deference and respect given to their views. They are merely *primus inter pares.* So it may be with the Pokot. Wealth is not merely the cattle held in one's herd. More intangibly and effectively it is one's ability to mobilize resources held by others through established relationships. In many groups, such as the Iraqw of Tanganyika described by E. H. Winter,[25] cattle are lent out as a means of distributing the herd, but also to extend the range of debtor-creditor links which can be called upon in time of need. There is little difference in principle between this and lending blankets in the potlatch at interest.

Such societies place cattle in a central ritual position, so that a considerable body of mythology, belief, and ethical practice centers upon them. Their role in establishing social relations meant, in practice, that the ethically approved exchanges were contained within the ethically approved society. Methods of obtaining cattle across sociopolitical boundaries were not normally through trade or exchange but by raiding and warfare. Winter points out that even where major ecological dif-

---

[24] Schneider, "Subsistence Role of Cattle," p. 281.
[25] E. H. Winter, "Livestock Markets among the Iraqw of Northern Tanganyika," in Paul Bohannan and George Dalton, *Markets in Africa*, pp. 457-68.

ferences separated agricultural from pastoral societies, trade did not develop, except on a very small scale.

Something of this position has carried over into the modern world. Among the Plateau Tonga, selling cattle for cash is considered quite unethical. This, after all, does not establish a continuing social relationship. Among the Iraqw the development of markets has been held back to some extent by the notion that a ritually impure person can contaminate goods and hence the recipient. To sell cattle through barter, for example for grain, would mean that the recipient of grain would fear to use it unless he knew that there was no reason for suspecting ritual impurity. Yet perhaps the entry of cash as a depersonalized medium of exchange can reduce such fears. Among the Pokot, goats and sheep are used in trade exchange more frequently than cattle, probably because they represent, as Schneider puts it, a smaller denomination of currency. (This, as we have seen, is a common consideration restricting the use of ceremonial objects in exchange.)

Despite such considerations, large-scale market trade is in fact developing. Let me quote at length from Elizabeth Colson on the Tonga:

> The Tonga are eager to buy from each other, either to build up their own herds, or for re-sale to European buyers on the railway line, or to slaughter themselves. The competition between Europeans and Tonga probably plays its part in keeping up the price of stock, and as the Tonga have received more and more money with the increased price of their maize in recent years they have had the cash to develop considerable internal trade in cattle. . . . In 1948, 4,563 head of stock were purchased in the reserves under permit by European cattle buyers, local butcheries, and farmers. . . . Men buy up old stock which they slaughter. They trade the meat for maize and then dispose of the maize at a profit at the buying stations. . . . Even a portion of the meat killed for a puberty ceremony or a funeral may find its way into the market if the owner decided that a whole animal is too much to sacrifice to his social obligations. It is therefore quite possible today for a man to invest in cattle, get the full value from the beast in the form of work or calves, and then recoup himself for his original investment by slaughtering the animal when it can work no more and selling the meat. Progressive Tonga are well aware of these possibilities, and consider cattle a good investment for their spare funds.[26]

It is quite obvious that ethical belief is not standing in the way of adjustments towards a cash economy. Similarly, the Iraqw have developed a major cattle market system upon which they depend (rather than upon agriculture or employment) for the major monetary resources of their society.

[26] Colson, "The Role of Cattle," pp. 28-29.

AN OVERVIEW OF MELANESIAN EXCHANGE

In the previous examples we have examined a selection of highly complicated ceremonialized institutions from Oceania, North America, and Africa. Although the details vary considerably from culture to culture, the main variables are remarkably consistent. These include emphases on relationships between individuals which are also seen as relationships between groups, and upon gaining advantages which can be expressed as prestige as well as in material ways, and with greater or lesser degrees of competition and rivalry.

Attention given to such dramatic and intriguing systems might leave the impression that these are the primary forms of nonmonetized exchange, and that they are in fact the economy. Such an impression may be reinforced by the technical difficulty of obtaining quantitative data about other aspects of production and distribution. An anthropologist who sees a ceremonial in progress has a specific event to examine. But when each member of a village is going about his everyday business working in scattered agricultural plots, visiting neighbors, making social contact in many directions at many hours, it is extremely difficult to arrive at quantitative estimates of different kinds of transactions. Analysis is thus usually forced to rely on general observation, and even here is sometimes limited because, as with both Malinowski and Boas, the anthropologist may find such things too trivial or troublesome to record.

We may put matters in perspective a little, however, by returning to the Melanesian scene and putting together the known principles by which the economy operates. First, it should be noted that Melanesian societies, and their neighboring Papuan societies (which can be treated together for this purpose), are small in scale, with seldom more than five or six thousand persons in one linguistic and cultural group.

A primary point to note is that a very high proportion of social contacts between adults is accompanied by gift-giving. Between friends who visit one another or who meet on a path, this may amount to little more than proferring an areca nut or piece of tobacco, much as we might offer a cigarette, but with a more definite expectation that it will be done. If the purpose of the visit is a little more serious, or if it is to be extended, the gift may be of food, and certainly a host will offer meals. In some parts, as in Fiji and the Trobriands, a visitor from one village to another will offer a ceremonial gift. In Fiji, this is normally a small bunch of *yaqona,* or *piper methysticum,* from which the ceremonial drink is made. It is always reciprocated by proffering a bowl of *yaqona* made up for drinking, with speech of honor and welcome.

Reciprocal gift-giving of this kind provides considerable opportunity for the recognition of rank, which in Melanesia is achieved social status and recognition as the representative of a social group of high or lower power. The giving is then manipulated in two ways, that is, according to the status of the groups involved, and according to the significance of the social transaction which the gifts accompany. In most of Melanesia, this will govern whether the gift be small and token, whether it be bundles of food, or whether it include ceremonial artifacts such as those which figure in the *kula*.

Fiji has one of the most complex and manipulable sets of practices in this connection. The small-scale gifts between ordinary persons visiting are magnified into vast exchanges on occasion. When an important leader moves through the country or when a party travels formally from one village to another, they will be stopped at intervening points to receive honor. At the edge of villages they exchange whales' teeth, and they are served *yaqona* with high ceremony. If a man wishes to ask for the use of a piece of land, negotiate a marriage, or enter into a partnership in production, a whale's tooth will figure in his presentation.

The transition from this to (1) trading partnerships and (2) complex ceremonial exchange is straightforward. A trading partner is simply a man whom one visits in another social group, and gifts must seal the relationship. Ceremonial exchange consists of gifts between members of differing social groups made much more elaborate in scale. Papua and Melanesia have many institutions which stem from these categories, including the potlatch-style shell exchange of Rossel Island and pigs' tusk exchange of Malekula, the competitive pig accumulation and distribution of central New Guinea and many other areas, the coast trading expeditions of the Motu, the ceremonial ring of the Loyalty Islands, marriage exchange in New Caledonia, and a "silent exchange" in New Caledonia accompanied by festivity and dancing.

Such institutions serve as focal interests for public life and in a real sense motivate production and activity. In the first place they call for elaborate artifacts which must be produced by specialists. They also require, in many instances, supporting capital equipment of some value, such as trading canoes. These too must be produced by specialists. In both instances the specialists may be located in differentiated villages, as well as being particularly skilled individuals. Thus there are villages of the coast of Malaita in the Solomons which concentrate on the production of ceremonial shell necklaces, using these to increase their supply of food, since they have few agricultural resources. They have to fish the shell in territory belonging to yet other groups, by special arrangement. In Fiji (and many other areas) there are inland people specializing in the production of uniquely designed cooking pots which figure highly in marriage exchange. Ware Island off the southwest coast of Papua must import all its canoes from communities which have the forest resources and skills. Such examples may be multiplied to cover the whole territory.

Such production is direct, for a specific known person who has asked for the product, or to carry on a specific trading expedition to a particular community with which one has a long-standing supply arrangement. It is extremely rare (though by no means unknown) to find a producer hawking wares which he has made speculatively. Such directness is in considerable contrast to speculative production and roundaboutness in capitalist society; it is complemented by the complete production of an item rather than of components. Except possibly in the case of some shell-bead manufacturers, one does not find accumulated speculative stockpiles lasting over from one season to another.

This may be a function of the relative lack of liquidity of manufactured goods, derived from the specificity of their use. In traditional times Motu women did manufacture thousands of clay pots, which their men took away on seasonal trading expeditions, returning with large cargoes of sago and many additional canoe hulls. But they always went to the same communities, social relationships and trading partners were established permanently, exchange ratios were standard, and there was a *kula*-like quality. Through additional smaller exchanges and gifts, the pots spread inland. Indeed, the whole coast of New Guinea consists of a vast lateral network of social links which channel trade, with connecting links moving inland.

Similarly, a high-ranking Fijian chief will accumulate over time vast quantities of pandanus mats which will have figured in presentations of many kinds. These will have been produced by many women. They will come to him because any transaction in which he figures will involve considerable quantities, and because the transactions of any of his adherents will include a presentation to honor him. But this is different from speculative warehousing. The mats will be redistributed on the next ceremonial occasion in which he has need to give.

The principle of production for a specific end extends into agriculture. Here it is a common practice for producers to allocate their produce as they plant it. In the Trobriands we have seen that this is effected by distinguishing certain kinds of yams as appropriate for ceremonial, and others for normal food. This is an extremely common formula. In addition, plots of ground will be allocated. A producer will say, for example, "This plot will produce food to be given to my affinal relative; this plot will feed the people who come to build my house; this plot I will give to my wife to dispose of as she thinks fit; these plots are for our daily consumption." This is a form of allocative planning.

The sum total of small transactions, particularly those within a social group and with specific categories of affines, adds up to what is known as reciprocity. Reciprocity is an aspect or quality of social relations. It is sometimes considered on the analogy of "one good turn deserves another," but it is more enduring and less casual than this, and may sometimes be accompanied by very strict accounting. Reciprocity implies that there are formulas which describe the patterns of expected cooperation between persons with defined relationships to one another. A man may borrow goods from his mother's brother or cousin and may provide labor for his garden or house building. There will be visiting between the two families, accompanied by food-giving and exchange of artifacts. Such transactions are remembered and known, and any default in duty will be the subject of recrimination. A man should be generous in such exchanges, but not so generous that he causes shame. These are "on demand" transactions which do not correspond to buying and selling in spirit though they have the same ultimate effect. Note too that a man may give a gift without its having been requested. To refuse to receive it would be insulting, but it opens the way for a later demand request which cannot be refused without insult or an implied social rejection. Thus I may give a shell necklace knowing that in six or so months' time I shall be asking for food to help in a festivity or labor for the garden.

Such procedures call for the exercise of considerable forethought and management skill. Every man of ambition in Melanesia is an entrepreneur. It is ceremonial and its marked exchange character that enforces this. If his son is to be married, he must forecast the time, plan his gift-giving and the support he gives to other ceremonials so that when the date arrives he in turn will have the help he needs. If he is to engage in competitive ceremonial of the *urigubu* type he must build up his gardens well ahead, thinking seasonally. One has only to watch an organizer at work in complex house building or intricate ceremony to respect the marked ability to manage intricate detail and complex resources.

If this entrepreneurial ability has a limited effect upon development, it is because of two factors in addition to those mentioned earlier. They are first, that concern with ceremonial channels limits energy and prevents it from operating in other directions, and second, that jealousy places a limit upon achievement and accumulation too far ahead of one's peers. For jealousy brings about sorcery and supernatural intervention, and a man who is too proud is bound to have a fall. But even here there are other sides to the question. Empirical evidence seems to show that where opportunity exists, ceremonial aptitude and commercial aptitude are not necessarily competitive, a man interested in one also participating creatively in the other. And the operation and fear of jealousy seems to be limited, so that where an activity is publicly approved the achievement is supported. Thus, for a man to accumulate food in a miserly fashion would bring disapprobation, but for a man to accumulate the same food and distribute it showing concern for his public relationships brings admiring support.

But we cannot trace through such effects on development until we examine the operation of such systems in the context of modernization. This is our next task.

MELANESIA IN A MODERN CONTEXT

Melanesia is of special interest to the student of development and modernization, an interest which derives, perhaps paradoxically, from the relative slowness of the changes which have taken place, and the relative lack of pressure to change. The islands are not in the forefront of world politics or economic empire; their resources are slender and little exploited; political and educational changes have been slow, largely because of lack of a resource base upon which to build. There are signs of a considerable increase in the tempo of change on all fronts. Nevertheless, it has been possible to study in various parts of Melanesia the adjustment of economies as seen from a village base, and to note the emergence of new forms of enterprise, and to analyze the ways in which Melanesian societies have used their adjustive mechanisms in reaction to outside pressures. Such an examination of the early stages of growth and modernization can tell us something of the nature of Melanesian societies themselves, as well as of the processes of development.

The Siane people, in common with other peoples of the interior highlands of New Guinea, were contacted by Australian exploration parties in 1933, but were not touched again by direct face-to-face contact until government patrols began limited regular work in 1945. Following this period, a Lutheran Mission has been established, and men from Siane volunteer as wage laborers for work in other parts of New Guinea. R. F. Salisbury studied these people in 1952, seven years after the first regular contact, and only three years after the first work party had left to obtain money for the first time in the history of the society.[27]

In his analysis of Siane economy, Salisbury distinguishes three sepa-

[27] R. F. Salisbury, *From Stone to Steel* (Melbourne: Melbourne University Press, 1962).

rable systems which are more or less autonomous, since there is no universal medium of exchange to bring them together. One is the subsistence system, which is concerned with the production of the ordinary commodities of life for families. A second is what Salisbury refers to as the system which relates to luxury commodities. These are seen as commodities which are used in a context of patterned friendship outside the kin group. The third is ceremonial exchange between social groups, which involves valuables of high degree. If we turn the analysis around, and start with relationships rather than commodities, and think of exchange as expressing or being part of differing qualities of social relationships, the Siane analysis fits the pattern we have already presented for Melanesia.

Siane adjustment had not proceeded very far, but a number of features are clearly discernible. One is that a considerable influx of goods had preceded the involvement of Siane in the Western economy, even at its limited level. The most dramatic expression of this was that steel axes had completely replaced stone axes. The entire process of precontact change was intimately connected with traditional patterns of friendship, marital links, and ceremonial exchange. Communities near centers of European influence, outside Siane, became sources of supply of increased quantities of valuables, such as pigs, shell ornaments (moving up from the coast), and the new steel axes, this being made possible through the use of cash income and increased contacts with more distant sources of supply. Communities such as Siane, however, away from the centers of influence, established trading partners or marriage alliances with those nearer the centers. Thus, women (and perhaps food?) moved toward the centers, and valuables moved out from them in increasing quantities. As Siane wealth increased, ceremonial inflated. Steel axes permitted an increase in production and made available extra time, both of which contributed to the enlargement of scale, both material and in terms of social relations, during ceremony.

Prestige tokens, valuables similar in concept to the Trobriand *vaygu'a*, are, to use Salisbury's terms, exchangeable to attain power. Cash has qualities similar to prestige tokens (lack of productive utility, durability, and homogeneity) and hence the Siane began to use it for such purposes. In the meantime another new commodity, trade tobacco, was found to have the qualities of durability and divisibility. While it had a direct consumption function, and a use in establishing and maintaining friendships, it could also be used as a store of value and traded for other commodities. Slowly, the divisibility of cash was also being noted, and its function perhaps changing accordingly. Other goods, particularly where usable in personal adornment, were being used to influence or alter the quality of relationships, as evidence of prestige or wealth was translated into personal appearance.

Some new utilitarian goods made sense in the Siane economy only through the introduction of complexes, in such a manner that one European good was a complement to another. Thus there was the matches-kerosene-lamp complex, the needle-cloth complex, and so forth. Salisbury regards these as representing a type of capital investment for consumption which was not present in traditional Siane economy. This view is somewhat doubtful. The stone axe and supplies of twine were essential to housebuilding, and houses were used directly in consumption as capital items; and one would expect to find small tools for such acts as peeling tubers, butchering pigs, or shaving. The principle of capital investment for consumption is present in most societies, though the concrete expression differs.

The people of the Southern Massim [28] inhabit the coastal areas and small islands off New Guinea to the south of the Trobriands. There are a number of ceremonial rings and trade partnerships which link with the *kula* to the north, and along the south coast towards Mailu and ultimately the Motu. In 1950 numerous small enterprises were operating in the area, following several decades of direct involvement in wage earning and vocational education. Numerous small entrepreneurs, sometimes operating for themselves as individuals, sometimes as managers of group enterprises, were engaged in modern small boat building, copra production, commercial shell fishing, commercial food and rice farming, and even in one instance, prefabricated house making.

Traditional principles of social structure, and the relations that underlie them, were all-important in establishing the form of the enterprises. In some instances, the work was carried out by lineages working under their own prestige leadership on their own land. In others, entrepreneurs made use of affinal and other relatives as sources of supply for labor, capital, and shell or copra products, and rewarded them by the distribution of cash, imported foodstuffs, tobacco, and other exchange goods. Subtle changes in the nature of social relationships were taking place at this time, but were not yet clearly discernible.

Further to the west along the coast of Papua is the Territory's capital, Port Moresby, which has been an administrative and entrepôt center since the late nineteenth century, as well as being the location of missionary educational endeavor. On the fringe of the town is a large indigenous community of mixed Motu and Koita people commonly

[28] Cyril S. Belshaw, *In Search of Wealth*, Memoir No. 80, American Anthropological Association, 1955. There has been a considerable growth in productive activity since this study was made.

referred to as Hanuabada. A study based on field work in 1950-1951 [29] indicated that there were considerable continuities in social structure and cultural values despite vast changes in the way of life.

Hanuabada could in no sense be regarded as a self-contained community, working out its destiny within self-contained social and cultural boundaries. Able-bodied males were almost all employed in the town in occupations which required a modicum of technical skill as artisans (plumbers, electricians, carpenters, drivers) or white-collar workers (government or commercial clerks, cooperative inspectors, compositors). Although wages were extremely low by comparison with the costs of minimum nutritional needs, wage-earning was the primary source of cash income. Because of involvement in the wage-earning economy of the town, domestic agriculture was at a minimum, except for certain ceremonial activities. By contrast to the Southern Massim, there was practically no development of individual production-oriented entrepreneurship, a situation which can be explained in part by the ownership and development of productive resources by Europeans, lack of capital, fears for security in view of town competition, lack of commercial links with the neighboring hinterland, and the relative attractions of wage labor and ceremonial enterprise.

Orientation towards the town in almost all matters of daily life in working hours implied the destruction of the time-consuming contacts with distant villages. Hanuabada is in an arid region in which agricultural productivity has always been minimal. In traditional times ceremonialized trading expeditions would take place with canoes visiting the Kerema of the northwest, bartering thousands of clay pots manufactured in Hanuabada for sago, canoe hulls, and other produce. Full ethnographic details of these expeditions are still lacking, though it seems likely that they had a *kula*-like quality. For the Hanuabada (though not for some of the neighboring communities) the expeditions have disappeared. Nevertheless, people from neighboring rural and coastal communities come by canoe to Hanuabada, bringing produce as gifts and for exchange. Some is sold in cash markets which have been set up to serve the townsfolk, but much is given directly to trade partners among the Hanuabada people in return for substantial gifts of articles of manufacture and for cash. Articles which still enter into ceremonial exchange come to the village in this way.

This does not mean, however, a complete decline in complex ceremonial life. Far from it. Wage earning stifles and fails to permit outlets

[29] Cyril S. Belshaw, *The Great Village* (London: Routledge & Kegan Paul, Ltd., 1957).

for the administrative abilities and competitive inclinations of the people, particularly since, at that time, able young men had not been given posts of responsibility commensurate with their talents. And although cash was not sufficient to supply minimal nutritional needs, it was diverted to some degree to increase the supply of ceremonial goods. Indeed, cash itself was added to the ceremonial objects used in exchange, and displayed along with arm shells.

It is not certain whether the number of persons involved in ceremonial increased, as has been demonstrated in other contexts, but inflation undoubtedly occurred. The resources and talents of the people became concentrated in high degree on the ceremonies of the life cycle which, as in other Melanesian communities, were concerned with competitive exchange. A marriage payment inflated, for example, from 54 units in 1914 to 546 units in 1951 and probably 1,000 units later in the same decade. A wide range of kinsfolk contributed to such exchanges, each their own small share, and the network of payments, receipts, and loans made it possible to increase the quantity of valuables available by increasing the velocity and extent of circulation.

Such exchanges involve kin linked lineally and affinally. In addition there are competitive exchanges, accompanied by dancing and festivity and involved food distribution in which ceremonial entrepreneurs gain prestige. The various sociopolitical units in Hanuabada and in neighboring communities participate in these events, contributing dances, receiving food, according to discernible rules which have much of the quality of *urigubu* in the Trobriands and potlatch among the Kwakiutl. While the number and complexity of such distributions has probably declined considerably, since they involve a full-time professional commitment on the part of the entrepreneurs, vast crowds participate, and they are a continuing outlet for otherwise frustrated creative talent. Further, they are the main motivation for agricultural production; indeed if it were not for them, it is likely that agricultural production would no longer be in existence.

The indigenous people of Fiji, the most easterly of Melanesian groups, are members of a society which is oriented in a more complex way to the commercial world. Most of the capital-intensive and technically advanced enterprises are in the hands of immigrant Europeans and Indians (the latter, mostly a peasantry, constituting the largest ethnic group in the Colony). The economic growth of the total Colony in the twentieth century has been considerable, based mainly on sugar, mining, copra, and banana production. Road communication and education in particular are two factors which have developed much further in Fiji than in most other parts of Melanesia. The Fijians themselves have not shared in this growth to the extent of other ethnic groups, but they have nevertheless been profoundly affected by it.

Fijian rural communities have altered the technical basis of farming very considerably.[30] Riverine valleys near communications are now largely engaged in intensive farming for cash crop production rather than shifting cultivation for subsistence. Market vegetables and citrus fruits are now common, bananas and copra sold on the international market, and bullock, plough, and tractor have replaced the digging stick almost entirely.

Fijian society contained within it many highly flexible and adaptive elements. Patrilineages combined, recombined, segmented, and separated to provide village residential and cooperative units, and beyond these to develop political and territorial groups with military power. Although descent principles governed membership in lineages and strongly influenced the allocation of leadership, the power and status of a lineage or its leader depended partly on its own prowess and partly on the alliances it could muster. Internal prowess depended on agricultural production and ritual standing, and above all on the entrepreneurial ability to generate and control events of ceremonial significance (I leave out of account here military factors).

Although many writers have stressed the patrilineal form of Fijian society, it is evident that alliance was the most significant factor in affecting the destiny of one's group. Ad hoc political alliance was possible and common, but marriage alliance was structurally the most significant. A man of position, power, and ambition came from a family with already existing affinal links of influence. He would extend or reinforce these through his own marriage and those of his children. He would manipulate the links thus formed to secure the flow of goods and services, on occasions which would always be ceremonialized. Power, prestige, wealth, and marriage went together.

In modern times, the principles still hold and are still valid. Western articles have entered into ceremonial exchange. In addition to the great whale's teeth which have pride of ceremonial place, the bark cloth and pandanus mats, pottery and the great piles of foodstuffs, the articles now include four-gallon drums of kerosene, bolts of manufactured cloth, and cylinders of salt made from raw material bought in the stores.

Exchanges between affines occur particularly on marriage and death. The number of persons involved, each on a small scale, may involve hundreds, thus combining into a vast network of relationships. It would

[30] Cyril S. Belshaw, *Under the Ivi Tree* (London: Routledge & Kegan Paul, Ltd.; Berkeley: University of California Press, 1964).

appear that inflation has once again been stimulatory, not only because of the increased supply of goods and general wealth, but also because of enlarged opportunities for communication. The transport system has made it possible to give effect to relationships over a wider range of territory than before with much more economy of time. Furthermore, difficulties of communication in the past (particularly through military hostility, language barriers, and the concentration of wealth in the hands of a few) effectively limited the manipulation of marriage alliances to a few well-placed families with the total support of lineages behind them. Today every family can give effect to some degree to its ambition, with consequent inflation.

The exchange acts are not however limited to the ceremonies of the life cycle or to the cementing of large political alliances. Cooperative endeavor is most effectively performed in Fiji when it is done for one social group by another, that is based upon an obligation to maintain one's reputation for action, upon alliance, and upon exchange. A man who holds a prestigious title requires a large building as his home, his ceremonial location, and a shelter for the hospitality he must offer on behalf of his group. The subsidiary social groups which support him must decide with him the extent of their efforts to bring about the construction of such a house. They, however, do not construct the house themselves: they gather the wealth of food and ceremonial objects with which to feed and reward and ceremonially recognize the workers. The latter will come from one or more separate groups, not part of the chief's adherents, but equal in status to them. Their participation will be secured by elaborate formulas of invitation, and a sequence of exchanges throughout the construction period.

Similarly, in modern context, a man who wishes to set up a farm can call on a group with which he has an alliance, particularly through an affinal relationship. Willing hands will set him up, plough and seed his land for the first time, erect his buildings. In return he will feed and honor them, and will support them when called upon. Or if he does not have land suited to his ambition, he may examine land in areas from which his wife or mother have come, and if it is better may lay claim to its use.

In these ways, traditional society has elements of flexible adaptability which Fijians have used to help them on the road to modernity. Unfortunately, the possibilities have not generally been understood in government, so that policy and administration have often countered them to their detriment, introducing a rigidity which explains the slow rate of change. Examples of this are the land registration laws which do not recognize the frequency and importance of the acquisition of land through affinal justification, and the dependence upon development schemes which do not recognize either the competitive individuality of the Fijian or the ineffectiveness of a group working on its own behalf as compared to a situation in which it is challenged and called upon to work by another group with which it has an alliance.

PRESTATION AND GIFT-GIVING

No word in the English language fully allows for the conceptual trails that we have been following. The interactions we have recorded are all part of exchange systems, but the forms of exchange are many, and the notion does not form a basis for classification. Rather, we see in the exchanges certain pervasive elements, which have been referred to as gift-giving and prestation. Both concepts contain glosses in ordinary usage which can confuse the analysis.

A gift is usually contrasted to a payment. The *Shorter Oxford Dictionary* says a gift is voluntarily transferred "without expectation or receipt of an equivalent." This sense of the word is not accurately applicable to the transactions we have recorded. In some instances there is an immediate reciprocation, and in all there is an acknowledgment of a relationship which implies continuous obligations and transactions. A more usual Middle English usage recorded by the *Oxford Dictionary* comes closer: "Something given to corrupt; a bribe."

Unfortunately, corruption and bribery carry moral connotations in our society which are not applicable to the societies and transactions we are dealing with. This point causes endless confusion. In a modern context, a politician receives a gift and promises to undertake a line of action; an employer receives a gift and employs a relative of the giver; a judge uses his salary to maintain a household of relatives and retainers. Are these gifts corrupting bribes? The answer is probably yes if the person who receives them alters his judgments and actions to obtain more of them for personal use. The answer is probably no if the gift is the material symbol of a relationship, the sealing of a contract, the payment for a service openly rendered, one element in a complex of continuous exchanges, or part of a stock which the recipient uses to maintain further social obligations. The accusation of bribery should be used most sparingly in contexts of development, at least until it has been demonstrated without doubt that the transactions were not part of an indigenous exchange network.

It may be questioned whether any gift is free of equivalence in the *Oxford Dictionary* sense. The psychology of gift-giving and receiving is outside the competence of this study. Nevertheless, some points can be made which indicate some remarkable similarities and differences between the events we have described and gift-giving in our own society. Marcel Mauss, who made the initial classical study of gift-giving and prestation comparatively,[31] has shown that gift-giving introduces certain emotive qualities into a relationship. Status and wealth questions are immediately involved, and the recipient must decide whether, and in what form, he must reciprocate. This involves an analysis of the relationship, the purpose of the gift, and customary procedure. One's *amour propre* is at stake and potentially threatened. A return gift or service or the spreading of one's power if one has superior status removes the threat. This is as true in our own society as in the aggressive potlatch.

It is sometimes said that transactions in our own society are impersonal, whereas those in other societies are highly personal. In some senses this is true, in others it is not. Much depends on the accepted definitions of personal involvement in the given society. A major difference in convention is that gifts in our society are given personally, to be retained by the recipient. Hence some of the connotations of bribery. But in others the gift is much more of an abstract symbol. It is accepted, perhaps even enjoined, that the gift continues in circulation. The person who receives it must himself share it with others, by distributing it or passing it on in some manner, retaining only a small portion or perhaps even nothing for himself. The man who did not do this would be greedy, selfish, or, if a man of status, not fulfilling his social obligations. Traditional societies could not in fact work the way they do unless the gifts circulated.

At this juncture we can see that gift-giving implies social imperatives, which leads to the notion of prestation. Here again, we must examine meanings and connotations, particularly since this term is not common in English usage. The primary meaning, again according to the *Shorter Oxford English Dictionary*, is "the action of paying, in money or services, what is due by law or custom, or feudally," which is very close to one of the technical French meanings, namely "*impôt communal affecté à l'entretien des chemins vicinaux et payable en argent ou en nature.*" [32] Such definitions imply a fairly clear obligation on the part of an individual to render something specific, the obligation being enforced by law or at least strong public pressure.

There is a considerable element of this in the systems we have been

---

[31] Marcel Mauss, "Essai sur le Don," *Année sociologique*, seconde serie, 1 (1923-24). Republished in *Sociologie et anthropologie* (Paris: Presses Universitaires de France, 1950). Translated as *The Gift* (London: Cohen and West, 1954).

[32] *Nouveau Petit Larousse Illustré*, 1948.

examining, but rendering unto Caesar is only part of the system. The potlatcher *creates* such obligations; he is making others render unto him in the future. A man involved in a reciprocal alliance network may not give or receive specific predictable items; time and need will alter the nature of the exchanges. Even a person engaged in *kula* or in bride-wealth exchange haggles, argues, negotiates about the quantities that are appropriate and acceptable. Manipulability, not rigid customary fixity, is a primary characteristic of most such systems.

But the notion of prestation came into technical anthropology and sociology in this context from the French, and according to Larousse its primary meaning is merely *"action de fournir, de prêter,"* which may be rendered "the action of providing, of lending." This implies that the actions in a prestation system carry with them obligations and expectations, but that they can be initiated freely, voluntarily, and deliberately. Although Mauss himself generally stresses the obligations and imperatives of the systems, he does introduce voluntarism alongside of these: *". . . ces prestations et contre-prestations s'engagent sous une forme plutôt volontaire, par des présents, des cadeaux, bien qu'elles soient au fond rigoureusement obligatoires, à peine de guerre privée ou publique."* Let me state again, though, that despite the force of social imperatives, Mauss has overstressed them at the expense of entrepreneurial and choice elements. Nevertheless, prestation being an uncommon word, it can be used technically if it implies an exchange system in which giving may be used to create social obligations.

It might also be argued that, analytically speaking, wealth in such systems is incorporeal rather than material. Notions of wealth in economic theory would not support my suggestion here, since although they are ambiguous they usually refer to a stock or flow of material goods and exchangeable services. Similarly, when anthropologists inquire into conceptions of wealth (let us ignore for the moment the impossibility of translating the concept into some other systems of thought, or the circularity of such attempts), they tend to be given lists of pigs, *vaygu'a,* cattle, ceremonial foods, and the like: the man who has these is wealthy.

But why is he wealthy? And why is the man who has stocks worth millions (even though counterbalanced by a similar scale of indebtedness) regarded as wealthy? Surely it is not merely the fact that they hold stocks of valued physical items, even though pieces of paper and not used in consumption. The man who holds the *vaygu'a* and the man who holds the scrip has power; he *commands* resources, he can call them forth at will.

In prestation systems, the principle may be traced one step further. The man who can call forth resources, who controls wealth, does not hold the resources in his own name necessarily. He has given the cow to another in a *tilia* relationship, he has given his *vaygu'a* to a trading partner, he has passed marriage goods to his son's affines. But having dispersed material wealth in this way, he has, through a capital investment, gained continuing control over future services. His command over wealth has been secured and has expanded. And he is known to have such power. This is the true wealth in a prestation system, and it is the mainspring of entrepreneurial activity.

PRESTATION AND MODERNIZATION

Systems of prestation may seem particularly remote and different from the institutions of the modern world, particularly to those who have been brought up with an ethos of individualism, or who begin their analysis of an economy with the theorems of economics. But has not our objectivity fallen victim to the inherent myths in our ethos? Could we not re-examine our economy, starting with alternative assumptions, such as that prestation might be its basis? What would our view of the economy and its working be then?

Unfortunately, no one to my knowledge has followed through this exercise, and many of the key elements which call for research conclusions have not been examined rigorously. Short of undertaking such research, one is at this time forced to speculate on the basis of general knowledge. Nevertheless, such speculation opens up some intriguing hypotheses.

It could not be disputed that elements of prestation continue to operate with strong force in our society wherever family ceremony is involved. One has only to think of birthdays, anniversaries, gift-giving at the time of a child's birth, and above all marriage and Christmas, to notice that there is an a priori case for the significance of gift ceremony.

Furthermore, decisions about the appropriateness of gifts include many considerations common to prestation systems. I recall discussing this matter with a large class of students. A few were horrified at the idea that calculations enter into such decisions: to them, gifts were free, untrammelled, without consequence. But most recognized the issues clearly. Gifts between fiancés are of a special kind, romantic, intimate, cautiously developed to test the quality of the relationship and to carry it further. Adults amend their Christmas lists from year to year, influenced by combinations of factors such as the imperatives of kinship, the intimacy of friendship, official and business links which carry a personal quality. Over and above these are questions of reciprocity. Would the recipient be embarrassed by a lavish gift since last year the exchange was a small one? Have we drifted apart so that I shall send a card this year, or will he be hurt because last year it was a bottle of wine? Is it desirable to recognize, through a more elaborate gift at Christmas, that someone contributed to a bridal shower or wedding gift? Does one strike a name off a Christmas card list because cards were not reciprocated last year?

There are of course major differences. The relationships are not based to the same extent as in other societies on affinally related lineages, with the expectation of continuing exchange between them. Nevertheless, particularly at marriage, affinal families do establish links of association and mutual support. It is not uncommon for them, for example, to work together to solve the initial financial difficulties of the new family, and to give later support to the children. Friendship appears to assume greater importance than lineal relationship; but it should be recalled that obligations within a kinship unit are themselves altered by affective considerations, so that the difference is not as great as might at first sight appear. And the activities of the organizer of a bridal shower are just as entrepreneurial as those of the person who makes sure that the appropriate kinsfolk support a marriage exchange in Africa or Oceania.

One has the impression that the direction of pressure is inflationary. This is a reflection of the general wealth of North American society, but it is interesting that as income grows, amounts spent on ceremonial gift-giving also grow (though probably by no means in proportion). It is also the case that on this continent the number of linked occasions has extended and appears still to be extending. The sharing of meals at Thanksgiving and activities at the New Year are long established in the same complex. Gifts have extended to Mother's Day and Father's Day and are now appearing along with the eggs of the Easter Bunny. Perhaps it will not be too long before Halloween turns into the same kind of event; already Valentine's Day has become the time for mass card-exchanging among children.

The cynics of course discern the deliberate manipulation of the commercial entrepreneur behind much of this, and can point to advertising and skillful propaganda as having its influence. This is no doubt true, but let us reflect for a moment upon its implications. The prestations of Christmas represent an extremely high proportion of total retail sales. Christmas selling is beginning earlier and even earlier to handle and expand the volume, and North American department stores are dominated through November and December by Christmas buying. Add to this the volume of sales related to other prestations, and one could conservatively guess that upwards of 10 per cent of retail sales are part of the gift-prestation complex. The entrepreneur is tapping a series of propensities of the ordinary citizen, and doing this effectively.

If the judgment of volume is in any sense close to being correct, the significance of prestatious giving to the economy is remarkably high. Further, it would not be questioned that an expansion of such giving, other things being equal, would have expansive effects on the economy, and be consistent with economic development. It is ironic that while this is acceptable for our own economy, the usual judgment is that the expansion of ceremony in Oceania, Africa, or Asia is inconsistent with development. Surely, such an inconsistency in judgments reveals little more than ethnocentric bias.

If the material in this chapter leads to a single conclusion more than others, that conclusion would be that prestation in itself or in association with other economic principles is consistent with enterprise, complexity, and growth.

Yet the societies we have concentrated upon are not traditionally examples of economic growth: they are economically static. If we rule out prestation as the governing factor, where then do we turn for explanations?

To some extent we have answered this question in our analysis of Trobriand economy, and the points can be generalized. The societies we have dealt with have been technologically simple, with few opportunities for capital accumulation in the form of a durable stock which would increase per capita production. The potentiality for increasing nondurable stock was severely limited by the supply of manpower, and it would not, in any event, have a multiplying growth effect.

There seem to be two ways of breaking out of such a position, and neither could be taken advantage of in these societies. One is to undergo a technological revolution. This leads us directly to a consideration of the sociology of knowledge, a subject which we cannot embark upon exhaustively here. But it should be pointed out that small-scale societies are limited in their conceptual vocabulary, that is the number of ideas, technological and otherwise, is limited. To innovate requires the recombination of existing ideas in new meaningful forms; technological innovation requires that the ideas be put to practical work. But if the number of ideas is limited, so too is the possible number of recombinations into meaningful practical alternatives. Thus growth and change are slow.

This situation can alter if ideas enter from other societies. There is some evidence to suggest that the scale of Asian societies in early history helped to create a growth in knowledge, and that in later years contact between Asia and Europe and a high velocity of ideational interchange within Europe contributed to movement. But for the societies of Africa, the Americas, and Oceania, this was not normally so. They were surrounded by other societies of a like kind, and although there was some contact between them, notions of ethnic and cultural identity, and limitations on the range of social intercourse, severely restricted contacts which might have developed radical innovation, so that development through the path of innovation would be slow.

Another type of breakthrough would come about through an increase in the scale of the society, implying by this the growth of specialized institutions permitting a more productive organization. This in turn could lead to ideational and technological advance, or it might be based upon some such advance, for example in military technology. The societies we have examined do in fact have some specialization of skills and there is some exchange and even trade based upon them. But they are heavily oriented to relationships between persons with similar functions, aptitudes, and skills. Every man can potentially do every other person's work, with very few restrictions of a political or religious nature. Exchange is, on the whole, of similar objects and services. There are very few specialized institutions, and these are not normally concerned with material productivity or trade.

An increase in institutional scale, related to an increased division of labor and differentiation of social roles, is an essential characteristic of economic development and basis for growth. The economy is primarily an organization for taking in each other's washing along lines which permit of increased effectiveness and capital growth.

Robert Redfield and Raymond Firth, each in his own way, directed the attention of anthropologists to ways of life which the former has called "folk" and the latter "peasant." Although the term "society" or "culture" or even "economy" has been applied to these ways of life, this is a matter of convenience rather than of concrete reality, since empirically a folk or peasant way of life does not exist in isolation in the same sense as did the societies we have described in the last chapter. A folk or peasant way of life exists as part of a socio-cultural system which includes specialized centers of power, knowledge, and wealth, that is to say noble courts or populous towns. Nevertheless, the way of life can be analyzed as an entity apart from the towns, since it so often exhibits a major difference in quality, except perhaps in those instances in which folk and peasant attitudes permeate the towns themselves.

Robert Redfield [1] stressed the homogeneous attitudes of the folk culture, the continuity of tradition, the dependence upon an oral rather than a printed transmission of knowledge, and a separation and protection from modern urban influences. In this, Redfield was largely concerned with contrasting folk culture and urban-oriented culture.

[1] Initially in Robert Redfield, *Tepoztlan, A Mexican Village* (Chicago: University of Chicago Press, 1930).

CHAPTER THREE

Monetized Peasant Marketing

Raymond Firth [2] approached similar kinds of culture from the point of view of their contrast to primitive cultures. Peasant societies habitually use money for a wide range of transactions, many of which take place in market-place situations. To this we may add the notion that peasant societies retain a high degree of subsistence production which does not find its way into the market. In this context, then, I shall refer to peasant societies as being ways of life which are traditionally oriented, linked with but separate from urban centers, combining market activity with subsistence production.

It should be obvious that the warnings about classification contained in Chapter One apply with full force to the rubrics "peasant" or "folk." The societies contained within the classification are *not* equivalent, even in the features singled out as criteria. There is a range of societies in which the force of the criteria and their implications are highly variable. This is merely a heuristic device to enable us to examine the variables comparatively.

It may also be argued that most formerly primitive societies have been transformed into peasant societies through the introduction of money and markets. Although there has been considerable study of the transformation from primitive to peasant as part of the process of economic development and social change, there has been relatively little study of peasant societies as such in contemporary anthropology and sociology, and with very few exceptions, almost no study of the sociology of marketing in such societies.

In this chapter we shall focus on the market as it works in the market place, and examine its links with the total economy and the society of which it is a part, to the extent that information is available. The examples will be contemporary, so that they will illustrate the conditions within which modernization is occurring. By implication, peasant marketing systems have forms of articulation with the total national economy, but the focus of this chapter is on the peasant culture itself.

THE MARKETS OF HAITI AND MESOAMERICA

Out of a total Haitian population of three and a half million, it has been estimated that there are 65,000 market traders, of which 50,000 are women. In addition, ordinary peasants, usually women, can enter the market to buy or sell whenever the need arises. A typical pattern is for a peasant woman to carry her agricultural crop toward the market

[2] See Raymond Firth, *Malay Fishermen, their Peasant Economy* (London: Routledge & Kegan Paul, 1946), and *Elements of Social Organization* (London: C. A. Watts & Co., Ltd., 1951).

place, disposing of items which enter the national economy, such as coffee, to licensed buyers who set up posts near the market. Her remaining stock can be disposed of to the professional or semiprofessional *revendeuses* or market traders. Haitian market systems have been thoroughly studied by Sidney Mintz and his students in a wide-ranging series of articles.[3]

The network of market places consists of a number of large permanent sites in the towns which act as major entrepôts and centers of accumulation of stock. These are linked through bus routes with up to 300 rural market places, some of which come and go with flexibility, depending upon seasons, the significance of the crops which move through them, and convenience to buyers and sellers. Typically, such market places will operate on one day in a week, the days of neighboring markets being staggered. This makes it possible for a *revendeuse* to carry her stock from one place to another, buying where goods are cheap, and selling where they are at a good price.

Role differentiation and division of labor are characteristic of such market systems. It would be hard to conceive of a market in which all buyers and sellers had the same crops and interests at the same time. One force in market systems, however, is that a seller can dispose of his stock at times when he has a surplus to his immediate consumption wants, buying it back at times of continuing demand but when his own production is not being harvested. As Mintz has pointed out, the market acts with a warehouse or storage function; but this is only possible if either (1) seasons are reasonably stable so that lack of harvest by one individual is counterbalanced by harvest of another, or (2) commodities are reasonably durable and some group takes on the function of holding stocks. Condition (1) exists to some extent, but condition (2) is more important in the development of trade, and is predicated on role differentiation between the producer and the trader.

Many traders operate on a fairly restricted circuit with limited capital and with local goods only. But the network effect of trading is extended by the establishment of other roles based upon modest increases of capital and the handling of stocks of more complex origin. Thus some

[3] Sidney Mintz, "Internal Market Systems as Mechanisms of Social Articulation," in V. F. Ray, ed., *Proceedings of the 1959 Annual Spring Meeting of the American Ethnological Society* (Seattle, Wash.: University of Washington Press, 1959), pp. 20-30; "A Tentative Typology of Eight Haitian Market Places," *Revista de Ciéncias Sociales*, 4, No. 1 (1960), 15-58; "Pratik: Haitian Personal Economic Relations," *Proceedings of the 1961 Annual Spring Meeting of the American Ethnological Society* (Seattle, Wash.: University of Washington Press, 1961), pp. 54-63; "Standards of Value and Units of Measure in the Fond-des-Negres Market Place, Haiti," *Journal of the Royal Anthropological Institute*, 91 (1961), 22-28; and C. J. Legerman, "Kin Groups in a Haitian Market," *Man*, 62, No. 233 (1962).

traders move stock between the urban centers and the countryside or between one geographical region and another, and others specialize in the handling of small quantities of manufactured articles. More daringly, others will obtain quantity stock from warehousemen in Port-au-Prince and act as wholesalers in the local markets. Each of these activities requires a different volume of capital investment, so that there is some correlation with wealth or ability to borrow successfully. There is also, by implication, some difference in the pattern of activity and of living: the contacts of the wholesaler, for example, are presumably more urban oriented than those of the purely local *revendeuse*. But it is not clear whether such differences are sufficient to warrant a conclusion that a differentiated class system is expressed through the market. Whether this is so or not, market transactions bind together the elements in the role system.

The point is reinforced by a consideration of regularities in exchange relations. The Haitians have a term for it, *pratik* (*pratique*). It is very similar to the trading partnership concept we have already examined in Chapter Three. A woman establishes a *pratik* relationship with a favored client by granting credit or a loan, or by trading with quantity or price concessions. There is no outright gift (indeed, interest may be charged on the credit), but part of the transaction is sufficiently gift-like to establish a prestatory sense of obligation. When a *pratik* relationship is established, both parties to the transaction have added security. They will trade with each other for preference, always at some price advantage: if goods are in short supply, this serves to smooth out fluctuations, and in any case removes some of the uncertainties of an uncontrolled market situation.

It is of considerable advantage to a *revendeuse* to establish *pratik* both up and down the market hierarchy, and with as many persons as she can handle with certainty. From the peasant farmer she obtains an assured supply of goods; from the wholesaler or from other traders she gains access to support, particularly financial support, when she needs it. Indeed, at an appropriate time, she can use the *pratik* connections to obtain a supply of working capital for the expansion of her work in some desired direction. Once again there are analogies with the reciprocal obligation networks of Chapter Two.

Such a market system works well when the requirement is for trading in small lots. This is the case in Haiti, since the peasants have extremely limited income and hence buy minimal quantities at a time. Furthermore, Haiti has one of the densest rural populatons in the Caribbean. Land holdings are small, and crops are highly diversified so that the producer may spread his risk. Individual producers thus normally have only small quantities to place on the market at any one time. As Mintz puts it, the poverty of resources leads to a trickle of goods into and out of the market. The whole market system is concerned with dealings in minimal quantities at the initial buying and final selling level, with only such accumulation as is necessary to secure redistribution.

It will be apparent that these market conditions (numerous buyers and sellers, division of trade into innumerable small lots, lack of major capital differentiation, considerable mobility of goods because of cheap communication and small packaging) represent a close approximation to the economists' model of pure competition. Were it not for the fact that even here there are characteristics which limit the pure homogeneity and interchangeability of the product (differences in quality, the effects of transport), this would be a good empirical referent for their theory.

All transactions take place through the medium of established cash currency, and by reference to weights and measures which. although archaic and in some degree unsystematic, do not hamper the effectiveness of exchange. Prices are fixed through bargaining in which relative scarcities affect the positions of buyer and seller. Knowledge of market forces is transmitted through word-of-mouth spreading of news, the comparative knowledge of other transactions in the market place, and adjustment to the degree of force exerted by a sequence of buyers and sellers. A major function of physical market places is to provide a facility for this kind of communication and adjustment.

Traders seek profit, and particularly the ability to buy cheaply and sell dearly. This they can do by buying from producers and selling to consumers and holding a continuous supply of stock so that a consumer can predict that he can obtain what he wants. Profit margins cannot be too high, since it is always possible for the producer herself to sell directly to a consumer: it is the holding of the stock that gives the *revendeuse* a slight functional advantage. This advantage can be increased, subject to the costs of transportation, by moving stock from one market location to another where price differentials emerge.

Since profit is held to a minimum, so too is capital accumulation. Indeed, it may be questioned, both theoretically and practically, whether capital accumulation is possible under conditions of pure competition.

But in fact there are modifications to the purity of the competition. As mentioned previously, one is that the stock-holding and transportation function of the *revendeuse* helps to specialize her role. Another is that human beings, except when they are dominantly attracted to the gambling excitement of risk taking, have an inherent fear of pure competition, with all its insecurities and fine adjustments, and the inability to take a good-sized profit except by windfall. They seek secure, patterned, contractual arrangements; they also seek, if they are enterprising, to take advantage of special conditions which give them an edge over competitors or a specialized function.

It is in this context that we must re-interpret *pratik*, for *pratik* introduces a pattern and regularity into an otherwise completely atomistic market. *Pratik* modifies pure competition by giving the transactors priority in the market. In *pratik* neither buyer nor seller is uninfluenced by market trends, but the force of those trends is modified, and the individuals concerned are shielded from their full weight. Paradoxically, although a *revendeuse* may reduce prices to a *pratik* buyer, the monopolistic element in the relationship may make it possible for her to work at a profit. For her as an individual it creates economies of scale, and in the market as a whole the weight of *pratik* probably raises prices slightly above the level which would otherwise be arrived at through pure competition.

Personalism in social relations makes profit and capital accumulation possible in a situation which would otherwise be one of pure competition reducing profit margins to a minimum.

The structure of market operations in peasant-oriented Guatemala and Mexico, as reported by such writers as Ralph Beals, Sol Tax, George M. Foster, and Manning Nash,[4] shows many local and regional variations, some of which show the marks of influence of the economy of the United States in recent years. But themes can be traced which show many similarities to those of Haiti, although the role equivalent to that of *revendeuse* does not reach to the same degree into every nook and cranny of marketing. In the *local* markets of Mexico, according to Foster, 90 per cent of the participants are women. In Guatemala marketing is much more a family affair. Men and women both take produce to market. In seeking sales, men rather than women venture to the town or far-off market places, the whole family visits the local markets, and husband and wife may divide their activity, each visiting a different locale.

A major difference from Haiti is that the responsibility for marketing falls heavily on the agricultural producer, who seeks out the appropriate location for sale rather than shifting this task onto a *revendeuse*. This applies particularly in the local market, but it also affects to some extent

---

[4] Ralph Beals, *Cheran*, Institute of Anthropology Publication No. 2 (Washington, D.C.: Smithsonian Institution, 1946); Sol Tax, *Penny Capitalism, A Guatemalan Indian Economy*, Institute of Social Anthropology Publication No. 16 (Washington, D.C.: Smithsonian Institution, 1953); George M. Foster, "The Folk Economy of Rural Mexico with Special Reference to Marketing," *The Journal of Marketing*, Vol. 13, pp. 153-62; Manning Nash, "The Social Context of Choice in a Small-scale Society," *Man*, 61 No. 219 (1961).

the supply of city markets, which agricultural vendors visit in an attempt to reach higher prices. (Sol Tax records that improved bus services have increased competition between vendors in Guatemala City, bringing prices down to a level which has discouraged many of them from continuing the supply.) It is thus the farmer and the small artisan who dominate selling in the market.

Role differentiation thus takes on a significantly different form from that of Haiti. In both Mexico and Guatemala there is a marked class system with clear cultural and wealth distinctions. Broadly speaking, one may speak of a Ladino stratum and a folk or peasant stratum, the former being of mixed ethnic, the latter of Indian, origin. Ladinos are by and large townsmen, small proprietors, and artisans. In many of the towns, also, there is a sprinkling of professionals (teachers, doctors, lawyers, and of course, the clergy). The impact of such class differentiation varies as between community. There are culturally isolated communities such as Amatenango, described by Nash, which have minimal contact with a superior class hierarchy, and which consider themselves to be threatened by and in opposition to the national viewpoint. Amatenango apparently does not have a local market. Other communities are class differentiated to a greater or less degree until one reaches the complex cities and metropolitan areas.[5]

Class differentiation is not solely a matter of wealth and cultural outlook, but implies also a specialization of labor such that the peasant is the small agricultural proprietor, producer, and marketer, and by and large other elements in the nation do the remaining work without personal agricultural production. The peasant coming to market, then, sells not to middlemen (there are some exceptions to this) but to consumers directly. The consumers may be other peasants, but the predominant feature is that this is the method of supplying the nonagricultural elements in the economy with food and to some degree with handcrafts.

Since the peasant is interested primarily in disposing of his produce and returning to his land, he does not often develop the role of trader as a specialty. Once he has sold his goods he may purchase consumer goods for his own use, but he does not in general buy things for resale; when he goes to the town he does not bring back small goods for trading. This function is carried out by small storekeepers who have shops close to the better established market places, and to some degree by market place vendors who come from the larger towns to the smaller. In Mexico the more sophisticated markets have some permanent vendors,

[5] A more sophisticated analysis of social differentiation is contained in Sol Tax, *Penny Capitalism.*

but in the less sophisticated ones and in Guatemala the presence of vendors dealing in specific commodities is unpredictable and irregular. Buyers thus may not be able to obtain what they want from them.

Nevertheless, the tendency is to obtain major supplies from the market places rather than from the store.[6] Perhaps, and here I speculate, this is partly because the atmosphere and methods of trade are more familiar to the peasant, and because there are price advantages. The small store, in common with stores in peasant communities the world over, is for small-scale and emergency buying. It should be thought of primarily as a retailing warehouse. I am reminded here of the functions of the Fijian storekeeper in rural Fiji. The motive in accumulating stock is largely to make sure that there are ample supplies available to the community when anyone has a sudden need for a small item and cannot be rushing off to town to get it. No one depends on such stores for their continuous staple purchases.

Prices are normally fixed without haggling for manufactured items which are found in stores and which find their way into markets, and Foster reports that in some Mexican market places such as Pátzcuaro barter is uncommon, although it takes place in others. For farm produce, haggling is normal. Sol Tax suggests that this is largely a reflection of uncertainties about quality and, as with chickens, size; nevertheless, rough measures are used. In many instances prices are unvarying over time, yet haggling is proceeded with until the standard price is reached, according to Foster. In others, prices are highly irregular.

There is a considerable variation in wealth among the peasantry, and it is possible for Indian peasants to become Ladinoized. The mobility that might come from wealth is not, however, as permanent and dynamic as might be expected. Wealth improvement is primarily a reflection of productive ability, either through small handcraft manufacturing or through increased land utilization. Manning Nash has pointed out that family unit manufacturing differs substantially from firm manufacturing in that the family depends on its own labor supply, which is severely limited, and does not use capital to hire additional labor. Its resources and expansive effects are thus severely limited. Similarly, individual families operating on land seldom have the capital or risk sense to hire labor to expand production, and inheritance rules and land shortage operate against the accumulation of land in any case. Peasant societies based on individualistic bilateral families are probably at a disadvantage in this respect by comparison with lineally-oriented so-

[6] A forthcoming study by M. H. Belshaw indicates that in Huecario the functions of the store have widened considerably.

cieties or those in which extended kinsfolk are normally called upon for corporate or cooperative ventures.[7]

But in Mesoamerica there is a further factor which often operates against the emergence of wealth differentiation in the peasant sector. This is the system which calls for individuals to hold certain religious and civil offices in the community which constitute an expense burden to them. In Amatenango, for example, four young men each year must hold the office of Alférez, in the course of which they spend more than the annual income of the richest man in hosting feasts and ceremonies. The young men are chosen by the official hierarchy on the basis of ability to pay; they cannot refuse the office; and it is likely to reduce permanently the assets of their family.

But the study of motivations among the Mesoamerican peasantry is not yet by any means fully convincing, and perhaps one should turn to the potlatch for insights and further directions for questioning. Indeed, Sol Tax has a passage at the end of *Penny Capitalism* [8] which suggests that this might be so. In writing of motivation he stresses the importance of security and modest better living (particularly to reduce insecurities such as ill-health). But then he stresses the "power to do favors and to give work to others" and mentions that

there are at least two achievements of high value that are attained only through the accumulation of wealth. One is rapid ascent in the political-religious hierarchy of offices. . . . The second is the ability to provide well for one's children.

But, of these goals, the hierarchy of offices, where it obtains as a significant feature, has the greatest effect on accumulation dynamics, since to provide well for one's children also means setting them up so that they may begin their status advance in offices. Manning Nash has made it abundantly clear that maximization of satisfaction is an operative principle in Mesoamerican society, even though the opportunities for the principle to operate are severely limited by resource and institutional factors. But if it does operate, it will be in terms of maximizing status whenever an individual *has a reasonable expectation* of being suc-

---

[7] Some confirmation of this is provided by the limitations of the bilateral mountain Greek family described by J. K. Campbell, "The Kindred in a Greek Mountain Community," in Julian Pitt-Rivers, ed., *Mediterranean Countrymen* (Paris: Mouton, 1963), pp. 73-96.

[8] Tax, *Penny Capitalism*, pp. 205-6. M. H. Belshaw also tells me that in contemporary Huecario weddings are more significant than offices, and that costs are shared. An *urigubu* model?

cessful in his ambitions. But as in the potlatch, status is attained first by accumulating property and then by dissipating it.

There are, however, features which make the Mesoamerican system probably less effective in accumulation than some other prestation systems. Specialization of offices results in considerable time consumption by the office holder, which withdraws him to some extent from production. It seems that the nature of the fiesta is such that consumables are distributed for immediate gratification, whereas in other prestation systems the articles distributed are durable and available for further distribution or delayed consumption. Furthermore the fiesta cannot be used to the same extent to create a network of indebtedness to the office holder, though perhaps this can be done in marriage ceremony. When a potlatcher distributes goods he knows he will receive a return later; not so the office holder in Mesoamerica.

MALAYAN AND INDONESIAN MARKETS

The rural and small town market systems of Malaya and Indonesia have been influenced profoundly by the colonial histories of the two countries, yet they have retained an identity which separates many of their features from the complex world of international business. These countries have had dual economies with roles stratified according to ethnic criteria, a feature of economic organization which will be treated in Chapter Four. Here we examine the internal peasant systems, which may be regarded as modifications of continuous traditions of exchange behavior.

The peasant elements in exchange can perhaps best be brought out for both countries if we begin with the implications of Raymond Firth's classical study of Malay fishermen [9] and extend them to the interpretation of other studies. This also gives us an impression of a relationship between productive organization and marketing.

Firth's study was carried out from 1938-1940 in fishing communities, primarily in Kelantan. The details of fishing activity show many variations according to region, season, and personal preference. But the basic organization is that of lift-net operations, which are linked to the technical requirement of handling a large square net with five boats, one for each corner of the net, and one for supervisory and servicing roles. The boats are owned individually (sometimes with shares), and crew members combine according to individual interest. A lift-net team may con-

---

[9] Firth, *Malay Fishermen.*

sist of twenty to thirty-five men, both they and the owners receiving a share of the return from the catch. The technical and business activities of the team are coordinated and controlled by one man whom Firth identifies as the fishing expert, and each boat has its captain. In addition, each team has a carrier agent who ferries the catch to the shore and is responsible for marketing it.

The share of the catch is made each Friday, the Muslim sabbath, although there may be complicating delays, when the carrier agent accounts for the sales and the fishing expert distributes the money according to the catch and participation for each day. One tenth of the return is set aside for certain technical needs. Half of the remaining sum then goes to the carrier agent. One tenth of this is held for his own boat particularly. The remainder goes equally to the members of all the boats, including his own, but excluding the fishing expert and those who have a partnership share in the net. The remaining half is distributed by the fishing expert, who sets aside one third for the net partners. The remaining two thirds are then distributed among all participants, the ownership rights in a boat being regarded in the same way as the participation of a man, including net partners, but excluding the carrier agent. This system of distribution, complicated and long drawn out though it may be, effectively rewards all the functional participants. Further, it provides a mechanism whereby the two important leaders, the fishing expert and the carrier agent, reward the participants and bind them together in mutual interest and confidence.

Confidence is in many respects the key to the system. Any crew or boat member may withdraw from a team; there is considerable mobility in participation. Much depends on the reputation of fishing expert and carrier agent, and upon the judgment of the potential participants as to whether the return to them is likely to be worthwhile.

The carrier agent is the link with the market. The most important agent has a defined special role with a particular net group. A few net groups do not have their own carrier agent, so that some wandering dealers may move about in their boats picking up catches for marketing. Sometimes the regular agent is busy selling one catch when another needs to be landed, so that a second member of the group may go ashore in a supplementary capacity. Essentially, however, the carrier agent is a full member of the group, specializing as market manager. Firth points out that there is some tension in the relationship between him and the remainder of the group, and that the fishermen refrain from slighting him or asking how much the return is for each day; social distance expresses the tenuousness of confidence and dependence. The role of carrier agent is not a partnership in the manipulable *pratik* sense, since each agent is a member of a team and is not in a position to extend and expand relationships.

The first market is on the beach. Here carrier agents are accosted by the dealers who begin to assemble as the boats come in, and haggling begins. The dealers do not bid against one another; one bids on their behalf. When a price has been arrived at (reflecting a wide variety of supply and demand factors), the dealers present at the boat distribute the catch among themselves.

The dealers are of numerous kinds. The nearby market is served by small-scale bicycle and carrying-pole traders. Others are interested in bulk buying for curing and for the export market. Others accumulate quantities which they take by bus to the inland markets, where they dispose of their supply on a wholesale basis to the market retailers. Firth does not indicate whether particular wholesalers are in a permanent relationship with particular retailers in a manner analogous to *pratik* or not.

The market system is thus based upon small-scale supply units reaching small-scale demand units with minimal accumulation in between, and with considerable role specialization through which the numerous dealers avoid direct competition and ramify throughout the relevant areas.

Michael Swift, in a series of articles, has provided a more generalized characterization of the Malayan peasant economy, in which the countryman depends more commonly upon the sale of rice, fruit, and rubber for an income. Exchange is heavily monetized, and even where, as is occasionally the case, direct barter takes place, it is negotiated and expressed in monetary terms.

But Swift points out that money is not used as a store of wealth, and there is little cash accumulation.[10] Rather, cash is turned into property, which is then frozen and hoarded. The most liquid form of property appears to be gold and jewellery which can be pawned readily, and which maintains its real value over the years of monetary inflation. Capital needs are met either by pawning, or by the direct sale of produced assets such as crops. If there is a complex capital need, for example for house building, the money will not be saved, but rather as crops are sold the materials will slowly be accumulated until work can begin. Presumably, this avoids the risk of dissipation of monetary assets for other purposes during the waiting period.

[10] Michael Swift, "The Accumulation of Capital in a Peasant Economy," *Economic Development and Cultural Change,* **5** (1956-57), 325-37.

Other forms of property holding are in cattle and land. Swift [11] is critical of the practice of investing in cattle, pointing out that it is an insecure and nonliquid use of capital, and that although a man can distribute the burden by farming out animals as in Africa, he soon reaches a stage where labor must be employed to herd them, and that the costs of this make the investment a losing proposition. Swift's criticism is not convincing without further data. Since cattle raising is a popular form of investment, there is surely continuous demand for animals, which would make it a more liquid investment than Swift indicates. If the butcher market is limited and if the Malay peasant must resort to paid labor to herd, returns may be limited. Nevertheless, cattle are an expanding asset through natural reproduction, and this feature is exploited in Africa, as we have seen, and in modern Oceanic communities such as Fiji. In fact, Alice Dewey refers to the considerable marketing value of cattle in Java.[12]

Accumulation through land is limited by the rise in population and inheritance. But even were this not so, there are limitations upon wealth mobility. The wealthy person must help unstintingly, but Swift notices that nevertheless he must pay for services demanded; there is a one-sided relationship which he feels creates a source of tension, and which Malays feel disturb the underlying balance of the universe. In older times, trading led to wealth mobility and the support of the status of sultans, who were, however, expected to be extremely generous in the distribution of their assets. Nevertheless, the existence of this dynamic should not be overlooked completely.

Indonesian marketing, as might be expected, has many points of similarity to that characteristic of Malaya, and, despite the confusions and misinterpretations of analysis which have entered the general literature through the writings of J. H. Boeke, is now better known through the more penetrating studies of Alice Dewey and Clifford Geertz in particular.[13]

The system is held together by extreme role differentiation, as traders move commodities to ultimate consumer.

[11] Michael Swift, "Capital, Saving and Credit in a Malay Peasant Economy," in Raymond Firth and Basil Yamey, eds., *Capital, Saving and Credit in Peasant Societies* (London: George Allen & Unwin, Ltd., 1964), pp. 133-57.

[12] Alice Dewey, "Capital, Credit and Saving in Javanese Marketing," in Raymond Firth and Basil Yamey, eds., *Capital, Saving and Credit*, pp. 230-56.

[13] Alice Dewey, *Peasant Marketing in Java* (New York: Free Press of Glencoe, Inc., 1962); and "Capital, Credit and Saving in Javanese Marketing," in Raymond Firth and Basil Yamey, eds., *Capital, Saving and Credit;* and Clifford Geertz, *Peddlers and Princes* (Chicago: University of Chicago Press, 1963).

One piece of cloth often has ten or a dozen owners between the time it leaves the Chinese-owned factory in a nearby city and the time it is finally sold to someone in a Modjokuto village who seems likely to use it. A basket of maize may be sold by a peasant to a local village trader, who carries it to market and sells it to a second trader, who in turn sells it to a larger market-trader, who gathers it together with similar baskets from other petty traders and sells it to a local Chinese, who ships it to Surabaja to another Chinese, after which it may begin the whole process in reverse in some other area.[14]

As in Malaya and Haiti, the differentiated roles are made up of varying emphases upon two functions, namely those of transporting on the one hand and of storage-accumulation on the other. The proliferation of roles and of numbers of traders is in part related to the absence of a safe, reliable system for the impersonal consignment of goods, which in turn is linked with the inability to buy and sell goods through correspondence. Similarly, the advantage of market place as against store under such conditions is that it permits the trader to move from one transaction scene to another accompanied by his goods, whereas a storekeeper must either close his shop or leave it in other hands while he conducts business elsewhere.

Local Javanese traders, lacking a kinship system in which lineage defines membership in a corporate group, use other methods similar to those of the Malay fisherman to establish cooperation. Dewey points out that some group formation is necessary to enable local traders to achieve economies of scale and to bargain effectively. The pooling of capital and skills in a group, membership in which is voluntary and mobile, means that specialist functions can emerge, so that within a group one member may buy from peasants, another hold stock, another conduct transportation arrangements, another negotiate with the wholesalers to whom the group sells, and one may explore the market situation in neighboring centers to test whether sales would be more advantageous there. In Bali, such groups have more formality and are sometimes based more specifically on kinship ties or a sense of social obligation and loyalty as between, for example, ruler and people. Nobles have used such devices to create large share-holding units, accumulating the small-scale capital contributions of peasants so that factories and department stores can be organized.

It is at this point that a certain difficulty in the analysis emerges. Dewey stresses the point that in a locality where most people are known to one another and there is much continual interdependence, forces of reciprocal obligation create a sanction system so that traders and peasants can

[14] Geertz, *op. cit.*, p. 31, based on Dewey, *Peasant Marketing in Java.*

depend upon the fulfillment of obligations, for example the repayment of debts. But where traders operate over a wider geographical and social range, and where their trade is mobile and free, such sanctions are absent, transactions must be immediate, and credit risks are poor. Geertz interprets relations between traders according to Parsonian theory, and holds that the relationships are specific (that is, specifically commercial rather than diffusely social), universal, achievement oriented, and socially neutral to the same kind of degree that is common in highly developed economies.[15]

The material appears to support Geertz's conclusions, but only if one recognizes that in highly developed economies there are considerable qualifications to this impersonal view of relationships. Relationships in Java and New York have much more in common than is usually conceded: this is the force of Geertz's argument. But both are based on the formation of trading roles in which there are significant limitations on completely impersonal mobility. The polarity of the Parsonian theory fails to recognize this, and thus leads analysis away from the socially important variables. (See page 80.)

The Javanese trader searches for the most profitable market. But, as we have pointed out for Haiti, if the situation were completely free and unstructured, there would be no profit. The possibility of profit first emerges through transportation difficulties and limitations in the acquisition of market knowledge, which puts friction into the system. But then we notice other factors affecting social relationships which are stronger in a local context, but which presumably have some bearing upon the wider scene. The first is referred to by Dewey as a patron-client relationship, presumably between Javanese and Javanese.[16] Here the rural peasant provides labor as it is needed by his wealthier patron, and the relationship is surrounded by other acts of mutual help, the patron, for example, being generous in time of need. The principle is similar to that which has been extended and used by Balinese nobles to create industrial or commercial enterprise, and Michael Swift has stressed the importance of the same kinds of dependence between traditional rulers and their people, sometimes in a context which in precolonial times implied trading enterprises. Given this background of social relations, one would expect that similar dependences would emerge where traders are in advantageous contact with one another.

It is possible to discern this, although it is not certain whether the interpretation is being forced unduly. The mechanism which provides a clue is that of credit. Trade is through the medium of cash, but cash is

[15] Geertz, *op. cit.*, pp. 46-47.
[16] In Raymond Firth and Basil Yamey, eds., *Capital, Saving and Credit*, p. 236.

in short supply. Transactions between traders are therefore largely handled through credit, the cash being used to establish down payments. The credit system does several things. It enables a debtor and creditor to establish a wide network of commercial contacts, spreading his risk over many relationships, in a manner very similar to that of *pratik* in Haiti. It binds the small traders to the large, and they to the larger, and this it seems gives an element of the patron-client situation. And, contrary to the much touted popular and scholarly opinion that holds that usurious indebtedness is damaging, it puts the debtor in a strong bargaining position.

This last point is extremely important. Sanctions may be unenforceable, either because the courts of law are ineffective, or because it is against the interest of the creditor to proceed against the debtor. This is the case where the creditor needs the business of the debtor. Both situations probably operate in Java. Furthermore, the creditor-debtor situation implies that there is a time dimension to the relationship; while the situation continues, both parties are in contact with one another, and the flow of goods continues between them. This ensures that both parties are established in the flow of trade; while they want trade, credit makes sure that it will come.

After all, is this so very different from the permanent trading links established between department store and customer through the exercise of credit? And do not customers find this to their advantage, even when expensive, since they find they can obtain special services while they are in debt, and that "account customers" whose credit is established are in a privileged position with something of a hold over the services of the store, and an entree to the facilities of other stores? And is it not true that stores are reluctant to take customers to court or to bring more than nominal sanctions to bear?

WEST AFRICAN TRADE

Those who have studied non-Western economies have known well that market place trading and itinerant peddling have played a significant role in many West African areas both traditionally and in modern times. Incidental references in the literature, and references to trading roles in towns such as Timbuktu, Porto-Novo, and Sekondi-Takoradi, have helped establish a forceful impression that market trading is a most significant part of the economic mechanism and that certain roles, such as those of the itinerant Market Mammy or woman trader of Ghana, are distinctive. Nevertheless, despite the crucial significance of marketing in West African life, studies which give a clear interpretation of its operation are few and far between, and are mostly collected in the volume edited by Paul Bohannan and George Dalton on *Markets in Africa*. The most suitable accounts for our purposes are those in this volume and elsewhere of M. J. Herskovits and Claudine and Claude Tardits on Dahomey, and the detailed yet succinct article of Simon and Phoebe Ottenberg on the Afikpo of Nigeria.[17]

Dahomey represents some marked differences from the systems we have been considering up to this point. In the first place, it was a unified kingdom covering a large and varied territory, working through a subtle and extensive bureaucratic organization. Central taxation was raised through levies on produce, particularly as it entered the market place. In addition the main trade arteries were controlled by toll posts at which levies would be made. Such taxes provided the ruling house with considerable revenues through which it was able to support a complex government. Trade was highly regulated.

A second difference is that the initial supply transaction is from farmer to wholesaler rather than from farmer to small vendor. While there are a few instances of producers selling their own products in the market place, and while it is typical for market women to get a start in the business by selling their own gathered products, in general wholesalers accumulate their stocks directly from farmers. They then sell to a very large body of retailers who spend their time disposing of small stocks in small lots.

The second difference, particularly, requires explanation, which must be speculative, since the literature does not treat of these matters comparatively. The first outstanding point is that in Oceania, Asia, and even Latin America, a very high proportion of agricultural activity is performed by the women, whereas in Dahomey it is performed almost exclusively by the men. In Oceania the traditional male pursuits have been warfare and ceremonial-religious acts, replaced to a great extent in recent years by wage-earning and political interests. In Dahomey the military and governmental tasks at least were undertaken by specialists as part of the political system. Upper-class women had an important role to play as guardians and supervisors of political and bureaucratic transactions, but the vast majority of women did not have such a role. Instead, they turned to trade on a large scale, and division of labor

[17] M. J. Herskovits, *Dahomey*, 2 vols. (New York: J. J. Augustin, Inc.—Publishers, 1938); Claudine and Claude Tardits, "Traditional Market Economy in the South Dahomey," in Paul Bohannan and George Dalton, eds., *Markets in Africa*, Evanston, Ill.: Northwestern University Press, 1962), pp. 89-102; Simon and Phoebe Ottenberg, Afikpo Markets: 1900-1960, in Paul Bohannan and George Dalton, eds., *Markets in Africa*, pp. 118-69; see also Rosemary Arnold in Karl Polanyi *et al.*, eds., *Trade and Market in the Early Empires* (New York: Free Press of Glencoe, Inc., 1957).

within the family was organized on the principle that men farmed and women spent much of their time buying and selling in the market. Since a very high proportion of women worked in this way (in one village sample, 176 out of 201, or 86 per cent), some motivations other than serving in the role of distributor of agricultural produce must be sought: otherwise we would have a situation in which Farmer A sold to a wholesaler who sold to a retailer who sold his own food back to him.

The rationale here is twofold. One is that the trading system provided a means of storing and distributing a range of products including meat and handcrafts, salt and oil, and, throughout known history, produce which entered Dahomey through the trade ports. The second, and perhaps more important, is that for staple agricultural produce, such as corn, the trade system not only provided for a storage system, but also for the possibility of making profits through speculation and through control over the market. The trading women are out for speculative gains based upon seasonal fluctuations and shortages of supply. It is this possibility that makes profit possible and gives a gambling excitement to the operation. (Corn prices recorded by the Tardits showed fluctuations of 300 per cent as between a high in July and a low in February, the fluctuations being all the more speculative since they were not according to a steady curve.)

A further feature contributing to the sophistication of the market is that since the women are away for much of the time, men are often in a position of having to purchase meals. Some women specialize in the production of meals in the market place, leading to a further division of labor.

The Dahomean system is based upon a long tradition, part of which was a sophisticated means of exchange before the entry of modern currency. This was provided through the use of cowry shells, which circulated widely through West Africa. There is a minor use of credit and of bonus gifts to promote exchange, and there is a hint in the writing of the Tardits that this introduces a personal link into relationships, and that the debtor is at an advantage. But we do not have a clear delineation of trading relationships.

The social structure of the Afikpo Ibo is very different from that of Dahomey. Traditionally, there was no state system, but a crisscrossing of age sets and patrilineages and a regional organization of village groups without centralized political authority. Men and women shared agricultural duties, and men were involved in military and ritual roles. Both men and women entered the market, which, around the turn of the century, took place on special days during which there was a general respite from agricultural work.

Trading methods involved barter rather than a medium of exchange, although valuable brass and copper rods did serve for highly expensive transactions. Despite this, trade was brisk, involving a wide variety of products, including pottery, metal work, mats, chalk, salt, dried fish, and agricultural produce.

Several trading roles were differentiated. Local producers sold their own wares in the markets of their village group. Some, mainly women, took produce to the markets of other village groups, keeping together to increase security. There is no indication of whether such market women accumulated the produce of others by buying from them for this purpose, but it is clear that the Dahomean role of wholesaler was absent, and the Afikpo system had much more in common with what we have described for Southeast Asia. In addition, one group of Ibo, known as Aro, specialized in a middleman's role. The Aro developed early as slave traders, and their caravans supplied the markets of the Ibo, including Afikpo, with manufactures obtained from the ports and from other areas of Nigeria. In this way iron, cloth, liquor and gunpowder from Europe, and native cloth and iron wares circulated within the country.

Discipline within the trading area was maintained through the operation of the age-grade societies, primarily as a means of settling disputes, and not, as in Dahomey, to raise taxes or in other ways to regulate trade.

The Ottenbergs have been able to trace with clarity the growth of the market system in Afikpo. Following the turn of the century, with the advent of colonial rule and the improvement of communications leading to an invasion by the Western economy, trade expanded and became more complex. Afikpo men themselves began to trade over a wider area and in a greater range of goods, bringing into Afikpo commodities from European centers and from other parts of Nigeria. Outside traders settled in the market place, presenting a continuous and secure retail outlet, in some instances operating shops which were open daily. Local blacksmiths had gone out of production, but their place was taken by men from Ezza who came to produce ironwork supplies for the market on a quasi-professional basis. But the Ottenbergs report that the main market traders were, up to 1952, still the small-scale direct producers. Cash had entered as the primary medium of exchange.

Other aspects of market development among the Afikpo were a result of direct intervention by government in the form of market place administration and regulation, a phenomenon which will be noted later.

MARKETING AS INNOVATION

The examples chosen so far in this chapter have been from societies in which market place trading has been a long established tradition. Even in Mesoamerica, the pre-Spanish empires were notable for the wide extent of professional trade, although essential details which would clarify the organization and system appear to have been lost to us. But in a number of societies where such trade did not exist in this form, market place trading has developed with the growth of Western influence.

There have been several factors contributing to this innovation, in such widely separate areas as Africa and Oceania. One has been the security of law and order which has made it possible for persons of differing tribal groups to exchange goods. Another has been the introduction of cash as a medium of exchange. The essential effect of cash in this context has been to facilitate exchange between persons of differing culture, in the absence of barter or prestation conventions. A third factor has been the growth of transport communications, making it feasible to move produce over greater areas, and to link producers through market places with the wholesale suppliers of the international market. (This last point has been modified somewhat, however, by the monopoly role of large firms in the import-export business, often by-passing the new market place.) And a fourth factor has been the growing dependence of producers upon agricultural cash crops seeking a market in towns where there has been a professional or specialized nonagricultural labor force.

The mode of change appears to be somewhat as follows.[18] Initially, forces of contact generate a demand for cash for such purposes as meeting head taxes, buying a limited range of commodities for household consumption, and for expansion of traditional ceremonial. This demand is met through the sale of wage labor for service in mines (Africa), plantations (Oceania), domestic service, and minor bureaucratic tasks. The growth of centers of wage labor, particularly in small towns and growing cities, creates an increased demand for agricultual produce available through the cash market, at the same time as the indentured contract labor system becomes less attractive to workers and indigenous peasants begin to compete with plantations for the production of export crops. The towns come to have an attraction of their own which becomes the basis of life for a permanent population, depending upon market supply for its sustenance.

[18] See V. R. Dorjahn, "African Traders in Central Sierra Leone," in Paul Bohannan and George Dalton, *Markets in Africa*, pp. 61-88; Audrey Richards, *Economic Development and Tribal Change* (Cambridge: Heffer, n.d.); T. S. Epstein, "A Study of Rabaul Market," *Australian Journal of Agricultural Economics*, **5** (1961), 1-18. See also Cyril S. Belshaw, *Under the Ivi Tree* (London: Routledge & Kegan Paul; Berkeley: University of California Press, 1964); "Port Moresby Canoe Traders," *Oceania*, **23**, No. 1 (1952), 26-39; and "Pacific Port Towns and the Theory of Growth," in Alexander Spoehr, ed., *Pacific Port Towns and Cities* (Honolulu: Bishop Museum Press, 1963), pp. 17-24.

In Port Moresby and Fiji I was able to observe the beginnings of marketing in new areas. In both places the first suppliers were peasant producers who brought handcrafts and crops to the market place, remaining there until they had sold their supply or reached the end of demand. In Port Moresby the markets had grown up without official regulation at first. In Fiji and other colonial areas, most market places are established by government, and the peasant sellers are subject to regulation and sometimes to fee.

In such areas the towns are from the beginning of marketing endowed with stores, sometimes run by large alien firms, and sometimes supplemented by small-scale entrepreneurs such as the Syrians of West Africa, the Chinese of New Guinea, and the East Indians of Fiji. The storekeepers themselves seek produce, but often are supplied by the peasant directly. In Africa, where distances are great, middlemen collect and supply to the stores, and as the scale of activity grows, middlemen seek out produce in other areas as well. In Fiji, East Indian storekeepers, truck owners, and speculative crop purchasers worked together. But as indigenous Fijian farmers began to produce crops for local markets, and as roads began to open up their lands to truck traffic, many Fijians themselves became middlemen, seizing the opportunity and learning methods of operation from the Indian precursors in the field. Many bought stocks from their neighboring Fijian and Indian farmers, and hired trucks, either singly or in partnership with other middlemen, to carry produce to the market towns. This was particularly appropriate for the supply of the more distant and larger townships; local towns were still mainly supplied by producers directly.

The reverse supply of goods into the villages was met primarily by the peasants visiting stores and market places, although in such societies village needs are still mainly met through subsistence agriculture. But both in West Africa and in Fiji the small village store has its role to play. This is primarily as a small warehouse of day-to-day supplies—matches, kerosene, cigarettes, soap, tinned foods, and the like. The store is a shack, a room, a veranda, and the storekeeper seldom has enough turnover to justify a full-scale operation. Villagers do not depend upon him for their basic supplies, but only for convenience. He himself, despite high prices, makes little discernible profit, since he can seldom buy in sufficient quantity to obtain genuine wholesale prices, and he has heavy transportation costs. What financial profit there is usually goes in maintaining stock as operating capital. The advantage to the trader is diffuse if anything: he keeps the stock largely for *his own* supply, and is at the same time willing to supply others. He has an intellectual or emotional interest in business activity (an entrepreneurial spirit deflected by social conditions from a more creative outlet).[19] His role in the total marketing system is very small indeed; his future, as marketing grows, cannot be predicted.

COLONIAL MARKET CONTROL

A major feature of colonial policy affecting economic modernization has been direct action to create markets where they did not exist before, or to regulate existing markets. In British colonial territories, for example, in whatever part of the world they happened to be, the administration defined market places which were supervised either directly by district officials, or indirectly through local authorities. Despite the almost universality of this phenomenon and its central role as an instrument of economic regulation, its general features have not been studied by social anthropologists, economists, or students of colonial government. There is, however, one excellent account of the effect of colonial market administration on a traditional market system in the article of the Ottenbergs already cited.[20]

In 1955 a District Council which assumed responsibility for the Afikpo market was established as part of the pattern of Nigerian local government. This change coincided with a considerable increase in the volume of activity, following the improvement and extension of roads and the establishment of lorry and bus services which linked the market more effectively with a wider hinterland. The market place itself extended from 2.7 acres in 1952 to 5.5 acres in 1960, and the Ottenbergs give other indications of a manifold increase in the numbers of traders. The increase in scale was accompanied by an increase in differentiated services. Bicycle repairmen, snack sellers, bakery shops, and barbers were either in the market or in sheds along the immediate access routes. Women traders, buying produce and processing it for sale, were emerging in their specialized role, and men were working in craft and service occupations. Liquor sales through nearby hotels, and other forms of diversion and entertainment, added an urban dimension to market life.

The agent of the District Council for market affairs was the professional Market Master, an occupation which is characteristic of the colonial world. The Market Master, with a staff, maintained good order and hygienic conditions in the market place. His role as settler of disputes superseded that of the age-set elders; in addition to settling disputes informally, he had the power, seldom used, of taking disputants or

[19] See Cyril S. Belshaw, *In Search of Wealth*, Memoir No. 80, American Anthropological Association, 1955.
[20] See footnote 17, this chapter.

offenders to court. Stalls were rented to traders and fees collected for the use of market slaughterhouses. Technical officials of the District Council controlled such matters as hygienic policy and market layout, and other officials used the market as a means of obtaining information and communicating with persons whom they wished to persuade. For example, the Government Veterinary Officer checked hides in the market and tried to encourage the growth of a hide industry.

It is apparent that the entry of an external bureaucracy into market place control created inferior-superior strata in marketing authority. Thus those in authority did not emerge from the village trading people through the growth of seniority, as was the case with age-set leaders, but through the creation of differentiated roles providing bureaucratic careers parallel to that of trader. The sequence was not now peasant, trader, elder, but trader, more specialized and wealthier trader, and parallel to this, junior bureaucrat, senior bureaucrat. The traders and the bureaucrats had differing interests, goals, and values and a situation of "we" and "they" emerged. In Afikpo this came to be expressed through the organization of traders' associations, which, though small and embryonic by comparison with other areas of Nigeria, were beginning to develop a common traders' viewpoint and preparing to exert an influence on market place policy.

The entry of bureaucracy into market place operations is worthy of further and deeper study.

MARKET PLACE SYSTEMS

In peasant societies of the kind we have been investigating, the market place is the focus and distinctive feature of the network of exchange which binds the economy together. But the peasant system of which the market place is part is wider in its ramifications, and we must now try to summarize its character.

One feature is that a large proportion of produce does not find its way into the market place at all. How high a proportion it is not possible to say with accuracy, since it is questionable as to whether monetary indices of value are valid in the nonmarket sector, national income studies are notoriously weak in dealing with it, and good empirical studies are so costly to administer that they are rare; so that we seldom have anything more than rough indications as to quantities involved.

The market place frequently exists alongside prestation systems, and may be interlinked with them. We noted this to be the case in Mesoamerica. In Fiji it is common for a man to earn money through marketing and spend it in stores on the purchase of whales' teeth, kerosene, and cloth (items not found in the market place) for ceremonial purposes, thus linking the three systems together. In Africa the markets we have described coexist with traditional systems in which lineage and age-set interests govern principles of exchange.

Much of the production for domestic, and some for prestatory, consumption belongs to the subsistence sector. In national income studies of Western society, economists normally adopt the convention that the value of suburban household gardening and self-help work is so small that it can be omitted from the computations. The value of services rendered between family members (for example, the wife's domestic services) is not easy to compute. But it is not a static or independent variable, since it reflects such factors as changes in the accepted roles of husband and wife, and changes in the use of appliances and tools. Sociologically, the neglect of this dimension reduces some of the potential significance of national computations. In non-Western societies, this dimension cannot be overlooked, and attempts are made to include it, since the subsistence sector continues to loom so large. But even here it may not be given sufficient analytical weight. For example, Indonesian statistics show a marked decline in food production as between 1938 and 1955 on Java and Madura. This may be an accurate statement, or as seems likely, it may inadequately reflect the volume of subsistence production, and a possible move of foodstuffs out of the cash market in this period.[21]

Another factor is that market place systems are today normally part of national systems which contain industrial and sophisticated commercial sectors which impinge upon the market place but yet are separated from it. These sectors usually do most of their selling through department stores or large firms with a network of trading stores and posts. Buying of staple commodities on which the export economy of the country rests is done either through the trading posts or through separate buying systems. This gives rise to the notion of dual economy which we will take further in the next chapter.

Thus, market place systems do not exist in isolation but are flanked on the one hand by prestation and subsistence, and on the other by a fully modern sector.

Most of the points one can make about market place systems are contained in the classical article of Sidney Mintz,[22] to which the present

[21] See Benjamin Higgins, *Indonesia's Economic Stabilization and Development* (New York: Institute of Pacific Relations, 1957).

[22] Sidney Mintz, "Internal Market Systems as Mechanisms of Social Articulation," in V. F. Ray, ed., *Proceedings of the 1959 Annual Spring Meeting of the American Ethnological Society* (Seattle, Wash.: University of Washington Press, 1959), pp. 20-30.

analysis is considerably indebted. Peasant market places facilitate trading in small lots, so small indeed that at one time, when currencies were introduced into West Africa, special coins were struck subdividing the penny into tenths. Buyers and sellers are innumerable, leading to conditions which as closely approximate pure competition as any institution other than some of the stock and commodity markets of the sophisticated financial world.

Maximization is a primary and valid psychological assumption. In the market place, this takes the explicit form of maximization of return, expressed in monetary terms. The peasant attempts to get the best price for his produce, the vendor sells at the maximum. But immediate short-range profit is not the only consideration the participants must bear in mind. Other motivations include an interest in trading as a speculative game, intellectual exercise, or creative act; the use of the profit to maximize other goals, such as those of the office holder in Mesoamerica; the maintenance of security in the exchange flow.

Profit taking would not be possible were it not for frictions in the system of competition. These come about partly because of the consequence of the search for security and the formation of partnerships, but also because of the functions of the market as distributive and storage facility. The market moves commodities from one person to another, from one differentiated role to another, from one geographical location to another. Communication and transportation are thus vital to its existence. Peasant society traders are capable of traveling long distances with heavy loads, of using every possible cheap means of conveyance. But the market truly thrives and come into its own when it can be supplied and linked to other markets by lorries, buses, or small boats. Expansion of road services appears to expand markets at a more than proportionate rate.

The storage function of markets is noteworthy. It applies even to perishable commodities, since it is an analytical rather than a literal function. Thus a man may sell eggs, chickens, or fish now, being unable to consume them himself, but by retaining the proceeds may be able to buy back similar commodities from other producers when his own production is in short supply.

This may suggest that the market is concerned with the disposal of surpluses, and that markets emerge where surpluses exist. This is far too simple a correlation. The notion of economic surplus [23] is extremely

[23] The literature on economic surplus includes: Cyril S. Belshaw, *Changing Melanesia* (Melbourne: Oxford University Press, 1954); Marvin Harris, "The Economy Has No Surplus?", *American Anthropologist*, **61**, No. 2 (1959), 185-99; M. J. Herskovits, *Economic Anthropology* (New York: Alfred A. Knopf, Inc., 1952); Harry Pearson, "The Economy Has No Surplus," in Karl Polanyi *et al.*, eds., *Trade and Market in the Early Empires* (New York: Free Press of Glencoe, Inc., 1957).

tricky, and it is doubtful whether it has much significance except in its meaning of unexpected windfall excess. Human wants, even in the simplest societies, are varied and must be balanced to make up a valid schedule of preferences. A man may not have enough grain to maintain his family and meet his kinship obligations to the extent that his values dictate: he has no surplus grain. But he may be in considerable need of an iron tool to enable him to continue to produce or to expand production. He may thus market grain, which was by no means surplus, in order to obtain the wherewithal to purchase an iron hoe from a blacksmith.

The market does not come into existence to enable persons to dispose of surpluses. It comes into existence as a function of the division of labor, so that those who concentrate on production of one sort may obtain the produce of others. Division of labor has economic exchange implications, but it is a social phenomenon. Societies just as materially wealthy as the traditional Afikpo or the rural Guatemalan Indian, namely the Kwakiutl of the South Sea Islanders, did not develop market places because the social system was not based to the same degree upon differentiated social roles, and hence specialized division of labor.

The notion of economic surplus is a red herring because only chance accident can produce a surplus over and above the planned expectations of the producer, who markets to obtain specific, needed, goals.

SOCIAL RELATIONS OF THE MARKET PLACE

The theory of pure competition posits a social system in which market actors are innumerable, and in which there are large groups of buyers who are interchangeable among themselves, and sellers who are interchangeable also. The structural relations between differing groups of sellers, and those who deal in differing commodities, and between differing groups of buyers, are not investigated.

But to the sociologist and anthropologist such relations are extremely important. Normally, the sociologist and anthropologist start investigations of social relations outside the market place. A class system may be defined using as criteria such categories as wealth, style of living, and status judgments. A lineage segmentation system is identified by reference to descent procedures, marriage rules, and the symbolic and legal definition of groups within the society. Existing exchange relations may then be clarified by reference to the obligations and duties of members of groups to one another, and interaction across the boundaries of groups.

But if exchange is thought of as a primary form of interaction, exchange patterns can define group composition, the relations between group members, and interaction across boundaries. Trade and marketing constitute one concrete form of exchange and hence give one major indication of social structure, an indication which has been underused by comparative sociologists and anthropologists.

Sidney Mintz begins the attack on this problem by reference to the gross categories of vertical and horizontal flow, the former being between persons in a superior-inferior status position, the latter being between equals. A market place system may combine elements of both vertical and horizontal flow, as in Mesoamerica where much of the exchange is between peasants, but in addition there is exchange between peasant and Ladinoized townsman. The folk-urban continuum is largely based upon vertical exchange relations, whereas the traditional markets of Dahomey represent horizontal linkages.

If, however, our interest in social structure is less taxonomic and classificatory than a step towards the examination of the workings of a system, categories based initially on status classification are of limited use. We need to be able to generalize about more complex maps which delineate the relationships between differentiated social roles. Little work has been done which would lead to schematic models of relations emerging from exchange, except where there are marriage links in prestatory systems. The market place has been almost *terra incognita* from this point of view, although the studies we have examined indicate networks based on role specialization.

The impersonality of the market place is an element in economic and sociological theory which requires much modification. Here there has been some confusion because impersonality in exchange relations has tended to be equated with rationality and the pursuit of profit maximization. To be rational (in the economists' sense) and to pursue profit one must ideally put aside all other extraneous considerations of an emotive character which create bonds of social relations which might work against the profit motive.

Yet one might argue, on the basis of the material in this chapter, that it is precisely the creation of personalistic social bonds that makes the market place system work. Clifford Geertz, in the passage already referred to,[24] sees that market place relations in Indonesia are quite consistent with profit-seeking and rationality, and therefore holds them to be as universalistic as in our own society, using the Parsonian dichotomy of personalism/universalism. But Sidney Mintz stresses personalism as against universalism. He writes:

Behind the operation of supply and demand, then, there is a network of person-to-person dealings which persist over time and outlast any single transac-

[24] See footnote 15, this chapter.

tions. . . . This personalistic background is not remarkable, and there are important parallels even in highly industrialized countries. But in the internal marketing systems of peasant societies, these small distinctions based on personal relationships loom more importantly.[25]

While I doubt very much whether such links are more important than the admittedly different ones based on the country club and interlocking directorates, the point is well taken. Geertz and Mintz have opposite interpretations in theory yet agree entirely on the facts.

The reason for this is that the personalistic-universalistic polarity is invalid in absolute terms. There is no such thing as an enduring nonpersonalistic relationship, and no economy in the world can be based entirely or even largely on nonpersonalistic relationships, for this would be the negation of continuity and security and would be atomistic group behavior rather than behavior in a society.

In societies with complex legal systems, those personal relations which are translated into enduring interactions between specialized roles in the economic system are often enforced or expressed through contract, and the contract can be applied to corporate entities irrespective of the persons who are at the moment in control. But the formation of the contract, its interpretation, and its modification are very much an aspect of personalism. Similarly, even in the absence of formal contract, regularities in relations between lineages have an enduring, abstract, and compulsive quality which is the social environment within which personalistic relations are worked out.

But in the societies we have referred to in this chapter, formal contract is weak, poorly enforced, or is present in the sophisticated rather than the peasant sector. In small-scale rural entities, binding obligations are certainly present and fulfilled, but as the scale of operation grows larger, as relations are entered into with strangers and members of varying cultures, traditional methods are often applied in new forms.

The search for enduring relations as a matter of confidence and security is a major feature of peasant market place systems. One set of links is between buyer and seller, whether producer-to-trader, trader-to-trader, or trader-to-consumer. A dominant manipulable technique here is the use of credit, which emerges as an important factor in almost all societies. There appear to be two primary forms that these prestatory-like relationships take. One is a quasi-monopolistic trading partnership, in which the two parties deal with very few others. The other is the attempt to spread the risk over many relationships, and to manipulate

[25] Sidney Mintz, "Internal Market Systems," pp. 24-25.

these to give maximum flexibility within a secure pattern, as with *pratik*.

Another set of links is between persons in complementary roles which can be combined into one operational unit, a corporate entity of some kind. This was seen with the Indonesian traders who combined to secure advantages of partnership, the pooling of resources, specialized roles, and scale of operations. This is indeed a microcosm of a firm, which began sometimes as a family unit, sometimes as a partnership. In Western society the firm is, in economics and law, a unit, which works with, against, and in relation to, other such units. But as a social phenomenon it is merely one way of coordinating roles oriented towards more or less specific goals. From this point of view it has much in common with the family, the traditional local polity, or a corporative kin unit.

LIMITATIONS IN PEASANT MARKETING

There is no doubt that some peasant market place systems are growing and to some extent modernizing, while others are relatively stationary, but precise global comparisons are not yet possible. National income figures do not on the whole help us, since, as in Mexico for example, we are examining one sector which is but part of the whole and not well distinguished in statistics. Further, it is not always clear whether movement is generated from within the peasant system itself or because of factors impinging on it from outside. However, whatever the origin of the pressures to change and to grow, one must ask to what degree the market place system can respond and provide a basis for growth.

There is little doubt that historically peasant market places have shown an ability to expand rapidly. The Ottenbergs' data on the Afikpo, and my own observations in Fiji, would indicate that market place expansion provides an essential outlet for an increased intensity of cash crop farming. It provides as well an opportunity for an increased division of labor and growing commercial experience, both of which make it possible for men to move from occupations in which they are less efficient into others which suit them better. The unwilling agriculturalist can become a trader or craftsman. Increased experience leads, relatively speaking, to improved technology and commercial practice, but it does not necessarily lead to the adoption of full-scale modern commercial conventions and institutions, which are still outside the ken or competence of traders, or which are founded upon high intensity of capital use instead of a large supply of trading labor.

The ultimate effect of market place trading upon per capita incomes or capital control, and hence on economic growth, is not clearly delineated. Studies of the emergence of entrepreneurs as modern businessmen out of the small-scale peasant marketing context, in Africa or Asia, are as yet almost nonexistent. The work of Geertz in Indonesia stresses the success of noble houses in creating capital-intensive business, but this has been less on a market place foundation than upon the skilled management of group capital accumulated by manipulating the traditionally kinship system. My own observations in Fiji and New Guinea, where market places are small and little developed, have indicated that the entrepreneur emerges on the foundation of specialized production, with little reference to the trading function. Market middlemen are growing, more income is circulating, but the change in scale is small, and as yet one cannot be sure of its force.

In part, such difficulties of limited growth may be traced to the relatively egalitarian participation of large numbers of traders dealing mainly in small lots. It is feasible for many persons to make small trading profits which are sufficient to justify their activity according to current standards of living. The large numbers, the strength of the competition, the relative weakness of the prestatory links which should create monopolistic frictions, combine to keep capital accumulation to the minimum. This in turn limits the internal growth dynamic of the system.

For a breakthrough to occur, several conditions seem to be necessary. One would be for a reduction in numbers of traders relative to the volume of trade, giving a trader a chance to achieve economies of scale. Sometimes partnerships may have the same effect. But the demand for a reduction of this kind is likely to be present in all parts of the peasant economy. For example, agriculture may become commercially efficient only if peasants leave the land, making it possible to achieve more rational land holdings and to gain the benefit of improved technology. A reduction in relative numbers might come about through a general improvement in other parts of the economy, leading to increased expectations of income, and making the act of trading less attractive. As some dropped out of the occupation, others could increase their scale of operations and gradually build up situations of advantage.

Immediate advantages to the alert can also accrue through the sudden widening of transportation networks, for example through the construction of a new road or the establishment of a new truck service. The scale of many market activities is limited by the absence or deficiency of communications institutions. Many peasant societies are even today poorly literate, and knowledge of commercial accounting and records is poor. Thus conduct of business by mail is severely limited. We have noted that the trader must usually accompany his goods from place to place. Although he can command transportation services, these are often not able or entrusted to consign goods impersonally. All these features reduce the scope of an individual trader's operations by introducing inflexibilities, insecurities, and a heavy demand upon his time.

Despite such frictions in communication, peasant market systems show considerable internal sensitivity and ability to adjust, although not to accumulate capital. Mintz refers to their limited articulation; but this is a reflection of their response to other elements in the national economy, rather than to their own characteristics.

A specialized political authority implies as a minimum the imperative channelling or coordination of some exchange relations. This may not be obvious in a diffuse and small-scale sanctions system, such as those typical of Melanesia and the early northwest coast of North America, but it is clearly evident in those instances where specialized instruments of political control, such as paramount chiefs, kings, and courts, can properly be identified. For the political authority to be maintained, it must have the ability to mobilize resources in order to back up its claims to forceful power, and it must be in a position to accumulate wealth and distribute it in order to maintain political loyalty, to reward agents, and to delegate functions. This makes it possible for political units to grow and to maintain themselves on an increasing scale based upon a complex division of labor. As the political boundaries are established, so too, in a certain sense, are those of an economy. For the political authority must control to some extent the external relations of its subjects, and these include those of trade. Such control is most sharply evidenced in times of armed conflict, but excise and customs posts play the same defining role. The boundaries of an effective polity are often indicated by the limits of the ability to raise levies, taxes, or armed forces. Whereas in many simple societies boundaries tend to run along lines of cultural differentiation, in more complex

CHAPTER FOUR

Approaches to Articulation in the Economy

societies the boundaries have a political administrative foundation.

This is not to say that polity and economy have always been co-terminous in the modern nationalistic sense (and of course there are important senses in which no nation is an economy unto itself). It is probably true that, except for states of deliberate siege, movements of goods and citizens continued to take place between countries which were at war at least up to the time of the emergence of nationalism. And there is evidence that strong political powers deliberately avoided encompassing free cities in order that they could continue to serve their function as trading entrepôts even in time of war. Sidon and Tyre [1] were early cases in point, Danzig a later example, and Hong Kong a contemporary one. The present-day notion of the duty-free port has something in common with the earlier free cities.

But to the extent that economy and polity do cover the same social units, one may inquire to what extent, and with what effectiveness or friction, the institutions of the society are articulated, or meshed together. For, as a very minimum, there will be one system of exchange relations concerned with the affairs of the polity, and another with exchange in which the polity is not concerned. In this chapter we will examine some of the variations in the principles of articulation which have emerged in specific societies. These vary considerably in their relevance to the problem of contemporary modernization.

BABYLONIAN ADMINISTRATION

Karl Polanyi has presented a new view of the operation of the Babylonian economy.[2] The traditional interpretation had it that Babylonia was a more sophisticated version of the kind of system we have noted for Dahomey. That is, the royal house controlled its military forces, its bureaucracy, and its empire by direct levies imposed upon producers and upon produce as it moved through the market. In the case of Babylonia elaborate records were kept which facilitated operations on a large scale and with great intricacy. It was known that there was a sophisticated private sector in which exchange took place through the operations of specialist traders, and it was assumed that there was a market which, as in the case of Dahomey, was the mainstay of the economy. Market and fiscal system in Dahomey were related through

[1] See Robert B. Revere, "No-Man's-Coast: Ports-of-Trade in the Eastern Mediterranean," in Karl Polanyi et al., eds., *Trade and Market in the Early Empires* (New York: Free Press of Glencoe, Inc., 1957), pp. 38-63.

[2] In Karl Polanyi et al., eds., *op. cit.* See also the article by A. L. Oppenheim in the same volume.

direct levies on the market: some such symbiosis must be predicated for Babylonia. Physical evidence indicated the emergence of peasant-oriented towns without market places, but with royal palaces constructed to serve as storage warehouses. The absence of market places was a central flaw in the theory of the Babylonian economy.

If Babylonia had been Dahomey, it might be possible for archaeology to work on the theory that the palace was also a center for social control with differing town communities having segmentary loyalties, but kept from violent dispute by the presence of royal power. The market place, being a center for interaction between communities, might then be in neutral ground, and not found in the cities at all. But this is a very unlikely eventuality in Babylonian conditions, and one must accept the lack of market places.

Polanyi's interpretation is at this point based upon a theory which is difficult to accept, although the conclusions appear to be valid and convincing. He notes the agreed fact that market places were absent and that detailed accounts of transactions were kept in monetary terms, but that, at least in early Assyria as in Ptolemaic Egypt, coinage was lacking or in short supply. The account system preceded coinage as a general medium of exchange. He then seems to argue that in the absence of the use of coinage as a medium of exchange, price negotiation of the market types is not possible, and hence Babylonia did not have markets.

This view is based on the notion of money as a functional entity having a particular form, coinage. But money in the economists' sense can be a quite abstract entity in the form of credit or entries in account books (for example, of banks). If it is used as the measure with which to balance up accounts, and the accounts are squared in a book entry, this is still exchange in a monetary sense, just as much as the exchange of physical pieces of gold. We have seen, in the case of Indonesia, that the shortage of cash coinage and even of immediate control over cash, leads to the extension of credit, and credit then forms the basis of exchange as if it were cash. Only the limitations of the accounting system and of confidence limit its theoretical use for all transactions. In our own society it is now possible to command many goods and services through the use of a single credit card, and it is technically feasible to control all accounts and transactions through the use of computers and a central accounting operation. The fact that Babylonian accounting was primitive and that it used abstract notation instead of physical coinage did not in itself prevent it from being a price-adjusting market system.

Yet though the predictive theory is not convincing, Polanyi marshals evidence which strongly suggests that prices did not change according to factors of supply and demand, but remained fixed, and that transactions were not based on price negotiations. It is this element of price fixing that gives the distinctive flavor to the Babylonian economy.

The model which emerges from the Polanyi-Oppenheim re-evaluation is as follows. The fiscal measures of the bureaucracy led to the accumulation of considerable stocks of durable goods and the development of a careful accounting system. Certain of these goods, for example, copper, were monopolized by the state, but since the producers of copper had to devote considerable time to its production, a mere levy would not call forth the production. The producers had to be rewarded, and this was done by guaranteeing a rate of exchange in terms of other produce.

At the other end of the social network of transactions customary equivalences governing barter exchange rates were in operation. This is a common mode of exchange in primitive societies and is linked with notions of what is proper and correct, which have some similarity to "fair price" ideas in our own society, though customary fixed equivalences are usually more enduring and sometimes less systematic. At any rate the fixed price of the bureaucracy was similar in conception and operation to the customary equivalence of the ordinary man.

Supplementing and linking these levels of activity, and subscribing to the same commercial ethos, were the professional merchants, who worked primarily on the consignment of durable staple articles on a commission basis. It is not clear from the account as to who paid the commission, nor is it certain whether it would have been possible to have two fixed prices, one at a trading post, for example, and another at the city, enabling the merchant to cover his costs. However, since Polanyi denies the existence of profit, this is probably not the case. For goods on consignment the merchant had to post security. Although he sold to the buyer for cash, credit with interest was available and used. The carriage of goods was performed by specialists who sold their services to the merchants.

The recording of posted security, of credit and interest, and of accomplished transactions was possible through the extension of bureaucratic accounting procedures. Polanyi points out that the system of fixed prices means that there was no financial insecurity to the merchant or to the state when the state backed the merchants or engaged in its own monopolistic trade (for example, the export trade). The search for security was carried further by an administrative system which made itself responsible for the actual price fixing by means of regulation and edict (though not for the whole range of prices) and which backed contracts with the force of law.

The agent for the administration of trade was an official known as the *tamkarum,* who derived his personal reward from land grants which accompanied the appointed office. All contractual obligations were registered with the appropriate authority, and it was apparently the *tamkarum's* task to facilitate those exchange processes which were indicated on clay tablets recording obligations. This he could do by guaranteeing the safety of money and goods, advancing expenses, acting as trustee whenever necessary (for example on the death of a merchant), and giving legal assistance. He was thus an administrator, warehouseman, lawyer, banker, and trustee, in one role.

This looks at first sight as if it were a highly administered system with each person playing a somewhat predetermined role with little flexibility. However, it is likely that the inflexibilities are overstressed, since in cases of this kind only the bare structure comes down to us, as recorded in archaeological evidence, and many of the subtleties are inevitably lost.

One such subtlety is of considerable theoretical importance. When we have price fixing of this kind, according to Polanyi's approach, we do not have a market, and we do not have an economy to which the principles of economics can be applied. To some extent this is correct. Prices do not change, and if price change is the index of the market, then we do not have a market system.

But this by no means implies that the forces of supply and demand are inoperative or that the motive of maximizing advantage is not a fundamental principle. When we have fixed prices, the equation between supply and demand is reached nevertheless. If producers do not feel that the price is an adequate return, they withhold production. If buyers feel that the price is too low, they buy until supply is exhausted, at which point there is clear evidence of short supply; if it is too high, they fail to buy, and producers are left with stocks on their hands.

One would expect this to have been the reaction in Babylonia unless there was complete state planning of every person's production and reactions, which does not appear to have been the case. But if Babylonians did react in this human manner, the position of the merchant middleman must have been a little less secure than Polanyi indicates. Except when the state was holding to a stable buying policy, the merchant would not be sure of his ability to sell, either to state or to individuals. What if the state decided that prices were insufficient? Fixed prices can smooth out many small-scale fluctuations, but when a large-scale fluctuation is in the offing they tend to hide its approach until a major adjustment is forced on the economy, in this instance presumably through political action.

Objectors to this line of reasoning might argue that it is based on Western capitalist suppositions which would not apply within the Babylonian ethos. This I do not believe to be the case. In primitive customary-price exchange systems there is no lack of adjustment in supply. And the same is true of administrative price controls under the differing conditions of the U.S.S.R. The problem is not one of lack of adjustment, but of seeking out the manner in which it occurs.

PORT OF TRADE ENCLAVES

Mention was made previously of free cities existing as trading entrepôts outside the boundaries of large neighboring political entities, serving those entities the better because of their standing as neutral territory where exchange could take place free of interference. The existence of such ports of trade raises questions about the nature of exchange links and the relationship between cities of differing kinds and their economic hinterland, which have not yet been definitively studied on a comparative basis. Reference to the port of trade here can serve two purposes. One is to draw attention to hypotheses which have been advanced about the nature of a phenomenon which, with variations, is of frequent occurrence, and which has historically been responsible for important exchange relationships, both ancient and modern. The other is to raise questions about the interaction between hinterland and city as a variable which affects both the form of the city and the propensity towards economic growth and modernization, and thus begin to link our study with questions of urbanization.

For our purposes, it is best to base the analysis on two recent studies, one of Whydah, the early port of entry into Dahomey, and the other of ports in India at the time of the first European contacts.[3] These studies are chosen because they show a remarkable similarity in the social organization of ports of trade at very different times and places and in connection with quite different cultures, the main uniformities being a mixture of political and economic interests.

Rosemary Arnold has shown that the port of Whydah was initially an independent trading entrepôt in a key position to export slaves supplied by a number of powerful neighboring African polities, and to

[3] Rosemary Arnold, "A Port of Trade: Whydah on the Guinea Coast" and "Separation of Trade and Market," in Karl Polanyi et al., eds., op. cit., pp. 154-87; and Anthony Leeds, "The Port-of-Trade in Pre-European India as an Ecological and Evolutionary Type," Proceedings of the 1961 Annual Spring Meeting of the American Ethnological Society (Seattle, Wash.: University of Washington Press, 1962), pp. 24-28.

channel European goods to them. The most significant of the African kingdoms was Dahomey, which, as we have already seen, was a centrally controlled state with strong military power and a complex internal exchange organization. But the Dahomeans themselves did not engage in international trade, leaving this to other more mercantile peoples. Dahomean trade contacts with Europe were satisfied if Whydah were an independent entity whose interest was to supply Dahomey and to export Dahomean goods.

The position changed with political events on the African continent. Dahomean neighbors began to receive arms, and it became imperative for Dahomey not only to obtain arms for itself but to restrict the supply to friendly peoples. At the same time the Whydans fell out with Dahomey and in the eighteenth century began to deny them access to their goods. The Dahomeans thereupon conquered Whydah and incorporated the town into their territory. It is at this point that the economic organization of the port of trade becomes clearly known, although it is evident that the form of operation remained much as it was during Whydan independence. Whydah remained a commercial entrepôt for the supply of Dahomey, which made little attempt to exploit it as a profit making resource.

Trade took place under conditions of strict administrative control. Importing was open to all European ships. Vessels were met on arrival by the Dahomean Viceroy or administrator, who negotiated with the foreign merchants the terms of trade for the imported cargoes. The merchants were quartered in the town, and their supplies, including food, servants, porters, and goods they wished to obtain, were included in the terms. The merchants were not permitted to by-pass the Viceroy and negotiate directly with individuals for their needs.

The terms of trade having been agreed upon, cargoes were landed in the port, where their safety was guaranteed, and customs levies were paid to the Dahomean administration. Resident European factors lived in various quarters of the town, all their local needs being supplied administratively. The cargoes were disposed of at the agreed prices either to the Dahomean administration or to Dahomean middlemen, many of whom held bureaucratic positions, and who were given the monopoly of distributing quantities of goods through the internal market places. The kinds of goods imported and exported were strictly controlled in the interests of the Kingdom. With few exceptions, Europeans or their agents were not permitted to travel in Dahomey on the grounds of the grave responsibility of the King for their security, and they were not permitted either directly or indirectly to trade internally.

Rosemary Arnold stresses the point that, although goods did find their way into the internal markets, the market place of Whydah was completely separated from the controlled external trade. It was a separate institution for the benefit of the local inhabitants. Europeans did not buy there or use its mechanisms to distribute their produce. It had its own hierarchy of officials in control, separate from those who controlled the import-export trade.

The Indian material, carefully marshaled by Anthony Leeds, provides a comparison which sharply focuses the main features of this type of port of trade. Indian political entities maintained the ports to administer foreign trade with maximum flexibility and security within the framework of strict administrative control. An interesting feature is that incoming vessels, whether from Europe, other Asian countries, or other political entities on the Indian subcontinent, established their social status and role by the donation of a prestatory gift to the ruler or his representative. The gift having been proffered and accepted, the merchants of the vessel became the responsibility of the port administration, their cargoes and persons were inviolate, and negotiations for trade could begin. To avoid the gift, or even to pass the port without offering it, was an act of hostility, and it was then justifiable for corsairs to pursue the offending vessel and capture it. There may be parallels here with the procedures of the corsairs of the Barbary Coast.

The acceptance of a foreign merchant into the port brought him into a specific role in the social organization, which he was expected to fulfill, and which made relations predictable, despite wide divergences in cultural background. Prices were fixed by negotiation, and embodied in treaties or contracts, for whole cargoes and categories of goods. Only those goods acceptable to the administration could be imported or exported. The administration levied customs duties. Foreign merchants were sequestered in specific quarters. They made their cargoes over to local middlemen, some of whom transported them to minor ports (sometimes at long distance) in local vessels. The merchants were administratively supplied, as in Whydah, and did not participate in local market places, even when they were resident.

Leeds mentions that prices are nowhere referred to in the documents as measures of market conditions, and in another more general statement holds that prices were a matter of law, and were not fixed by supply and demand fluctuations. These statements appear to be literally correct, but as in the case of Babylonia, the implication should not be the nonexistence of supply and demand or of price flexibility. Indeed, the references Leeds quotes liberally mention hardheaded (and dangerous?) bargaining, and the use of money in exchange. In reaching prices, no doubt, monopoly and power were important factors.

To sum up, these types of port of trade were based upon a number of social premises. The foreign merchant was assigned a specific social role by the political authority which gave his actions predictability and offered him security. The merchants' social contacts were limited to those with other merchants in the same or similar ethnic enclaves, and they had no direct impact on the total economy. Their exchange transactions were essentially an aspect of administrative policy, and the articulation of international trade was carried out through the bureaucracy.

The question now arises: can these principles be extended or amended to describe ports of trade under differing political conditions? The case we shall consider, since it is most pertinent to the context of modernization, is that of colonial port towns.

There were of course many differences in the administration of colonial port towns, and variations between them. The political control was that of governments which had allegiances alien to the indigenous people and closer to that of the foreign trader. Although non-Euro-American foreign traders except those of the administering power were often discouraged from trading through the manipulation of customs duties and other regulations, there was often a substantial smaller-scale trading group from other alien countries (Chinese in Indonesia, Syrians in West Africa, Indians in East Africa). The open door policy of the older trading ports tended to disappear, and the weight of administrative power changed in favor of the interests of the foreign merchant.

At the same time, other controls loosened. Protection of the merchant covered his movement throughout the country should he so wish it, and the merchant and his agents were usually free to buy and sell wherever they wished. The factor's warehouse became transformed into a trading and department store or commercial house, often with branch stores and trading posts at key centers within the country. Although this is by no means true everywhere, the foreign merchant tended to distribute through his own agents, or through wholesaling to other foreign merchants and small shopkeepers. The initial impact of the colonial society tended to eliminate the indigenous middleman and certainly discouraged his emergence where he did not already exist. Security of trade, to the foreigner, took the form of controlling his business contacts, if possible within his own organization, rather than operating through price contracts with the administration.

These are substantial differences. But other features of the port of trade system can still be recognized. While the articulation of international trade with the local economy was perhaps more substantial and more direct under the colonial regime (for labor and food were bought directly from local suppliers), the foreign controlled exchange was still an ethnic and economic enclave. It did not normally descend into the market place. Social relations with the indigenous population were minimal. And many of the colonial ports of trade (though by no means all) had minimal contacts with the surrounding hinterland.

A case in point is the capital of Australian Papua and New Guinea, Port Moresby. This town became the administrative and commercial headquarters of the territory. But the large commercial houses which established themselves there sold directly through their own stores, and distributed to branch stores established in a very few centers which were primarily minor ports along the coast. At least until 1950 or thereabouts, Europeans were the main buyers in the stores, but the firms provided wholesale goods to small traders, mainly European and Chinese, for sale to natives, and many of the plantation owners operated trade stores. These too were located primarily along the coast. Insofar as the overseas firms handled foodstuffs, these were primarily of overseas origin, and primarily for the European settlers or for rations for labor in European-owned enterprises.

The indigenous urban population was made up partly of Papuan villages caught up in the process of urbanization, a few Papuans or persons of mixed ancestry in steady employment, and a large number of immigrant laborers, most of whom returned to their homes after one, two, or three years. The food supply of the laborers was provided by the issuance of rations by the firms or individuals who employed them. Slowly, as the number of permanently settled Papuans increased, local markets developed. Occasionally Europeans bought there, but on the whole they were separate from the commercial store complex.

There was only one major road out of Port Moresby, which had almost no effect on the local economy, since it was designed to serve European interests, and not to tap the labor supply and resources of the nearby villages and countryside. The structure of commercial interests was geared to the international market, and security lay in dealing with other Europeans. Thus the plantations supplied export crops, and almost all commercial, industrial, and construction supplies were imported. Development of local industry was minimal, and the countryside around Port Moresby did not develop services or engage in economic growth, since the town almost completely failed to stimulate it. The European commercial sector of Port Moresby had more contact with the small port of Samarai, two hundred miles to the east, than it did with Papuan communities ten or twenty miles away.

Not all colonial ports of trade have quite the same extreme separation from the immediate countryside, or are so parasitic or neutral in their effects upon it. Suva, in Fiji, for example, has a much greater integration with the nearby rural areas. The network of roads leads to a much more intensive intercommunication, the established indigenous population is larger and has significant rural contacts, the immigrant Indian population has stimulated the establishment of small industries and commercial enterprises, both Indian and Fijian, and commercial firms make a greater use of local supplies (timber, for example).[4]

This material suggests two lines for further investigation. One is that the port of trade under free or indigenous administration is one resultant of factors which apply with differing weight to colonial ports of trade, and possibly to other urban units which specialize in foreign trade. Leeds attempts to give an ecological explanation for the existence of ports of trade, holding that they serve to link differing ecological areas. This is far too simple. There are strong forces of political control, commercial practice, and social relations which determine their nature, which further comparative study can elucidate.

A second line of investigation is prompted by the realization that the nature of a city is very largely determined by its external links. In dealing with ports of trade we have stressed the limitations on the exchange and therefore the social relations of elements in the population, including resident foreigners. These limitations do not mean that social relations do not exist: they define the social relations. But the social relations are of such an order that they create ethnic enclaves within the city's social structure, giving the city a special character. This in turn has consequences for the kind of growth, or lack of it, which will take place within the city. Such social relations cannot be analyzed adequately if we treat the city in isolation, but only if we see it as having outside, foreign, links, and as engaged in the process of creating social roles for such foreigners.

Similarly, the towns we have examined differ vastly in their relations with the indigenous countryside. Notions such as Redfield's folk-urban continuum, Hoselitz' generative and parasitic cities, and Redfield and Singer's [5] orthogenetic and heterogenetic cities, begin to draw attention to such variables, their consequences for city formation, and hence for urban-rural interaction, exchange patterns, modernization, and economic growth. But the typologies and variables so far advanced are not subtle

[4] Cf. Cyril S. Belshaw, *The Great Village* (London: Routledge & Kegan Paul, Ltd., 1957); "Port Moresby Canoe Traders," *Oceania*, **23**, No. 1 (1952), 26-39; and "Pacific Port Towns and the Theory of Growth," in Alexander Spoehr, ed., *Pacific Port Towns and Cities* (Honolulu: Bishop Museum Press, 1963), pp. 17-24. Note also essays in B. F. Hoselitz, *Sociological Aspects of Economic Growth* (New York: Free Press of Glencoe, Inc., 1960).

[5] Robert Redfield and Milton Singer, "The Cultural Role of Cities," *Economic Development and Cultural Change*, **3**, No. 1 (1954), 53-73.

enough to encompass all the cases, and there is still too much emphasis on the city as an isolated entity to account satisfactorily for its form and its degree of economic and social dynamism.

DUAL ECONOMY AND PLURAL SOCIETY

Until the new wave of theoretical interest in economic development came in the late forties, following the increased awareness of the dependent world in World War II, the two most influential thinkers on colonial social and economic dynamics were the English social and political historian J. S. Furnivall and the Dutch economist J. H. Boeke. Furnivall was deeply immersed in the affairs of Burma, but much of his conceptual insight came from his study of Indonesia, then Netherlands Indies, and his contact with the thought of Boeke and other Dutch writers. Boeke's original formulation of the concept of dual economy appeared in 1910 [6] and was accompanied by an article of Furnivall's in the *Economic Journal* in the same year. However, the classical and most influential statements were contained in Furnivall's *Netherlands India, a Study of Plural Economy* (1939) [7] and Boeke's *The Structure of the Netherlands Indian Economy* (1942) and *Economics and Economic Policy of Dual Societies* (1953).[8] Both writers repeated their viewpoint and even phraseology in numerous other books, Boeke in particular showing little awareness of the modifications to his theory called for by contemporary criticism and modern points of view.

It is curious to note that although the theories of both writers had almost identical foundations, the practical and political implications of each were vastly different. Furnivall, a staunch liberal and socialist who gave his career to the Burmese people, used the notion of the plural society to reveal the weaknesses of capitalist colonialism, to show that it did little to advance the interests of the peasant sector, and to open the way for other approaches to development policy. Boeke, conservative and pessimistic, was convinced that traditional peasant economies were so vastly different in their operations that economic theory could not be applied to them, that they constituted an archaic sector in dual economies, and that they were most unlikely to respond to attempts to trans-

[6] J. H. Boeke, *Tropisch-Koloniale Staathuishoudkunde,* followed more explicitly by *Dualistische Economie* in 1930.

[7] J. S. Furnivall, *Netherlands India, A Study of Plural Economy* (Cambridge: Cambridge University Press, 1939).

[8] J. H. Boeke, *The Structure of the Netherlands Indian Economy* (New York: Institute of Pacific Relations, 1942); and *Economics and Economic Policy of Dual Societies* (New York: Institute of Pacific Relations, 1953).

form them on the basis of modern suppositions. Both views are widely current today, and are represented, in more subtle forms, in most theories of economic development.

The notion of dual economy implies that, within one political framework, there is one sector which operates according to the principles of modern capitalism. This sector is commercially sophisticated, linked with international trade, dominated by motives of maximization, and in the colonial context, almost entirely in the hands of aliens or residents of alien extraction. Such aliens are primarily from the metropolitan country of the governing power, although others sharing the commercial approach to the economy, such as Chinese immigrants in Indonesia, are included.

Opposed to this sector and separated from it is the traditional peasant economy, which according to the puristic form of the theory, is conservatively oriented, interested in security and continuity rather than change, not concerned with maximization of profit or of resource use, oriented towards the satisfaction of social needs rather than reacting to international forces, and incapable of engaging dynamically in trade and commerce. Except for a very small minority of Westernized natives who have left traditional society, the indigenous population lies in this sector.

The puristic form of the theory held that there was minimal interaction between these two sectors, and that the example of the commercial sector did not lead to innovation in the traditional one. There were two worlds, quite separate, and the separateness was reinforced by quite different cultural values held by the ethnically distinct populations.

There was much to support this view, which implied that there was no articulation of the institutions of the society as a whole, but only within the two separate systems. It could be cited, for example, that plantation agriculture was oriented to the commercial sector and had little demonstration effect, or any other effect, on the practices of the peasant population in such countries as New Guinea. And there was the material we have examined for ports of trade and colonial towns, which reinforces the idea of separateness. But the model was too simplistic and easily demolished, although Boeke held to it tenaciously, and there are echoes of it in Redfield's folk-urban continuum.

In the first place, the characterization of primitive and peasant societies as being uninterested in maximization is demonstrably false. We have shown this to be the case in terms of their own values. If there is a distinction, it is because maximization is of different things, with different values, and using different methods.

But once it is admitted that the difference is not between maximization and nonmaximization, but between different *kinds* of maximization, the distinctions can be not between just two sectors but between many sectors, that is between all subcultures. This is partly Furnivall's point, and is the reason for his preferring the concept of *plural* society. A plural society is one in which the values held by the several population components are such that they lack a central political loyalty which overrules sectional interests, and they lack social and cultural homogeneity or even a basis of understanding. The groups thus separated have differing modes of organization, reflected in the economy, and they have differing roles to play in the economy. Society and economy are held together, in different historical epochs, by the assignment of roles through a caste-like hierarchy, by the imposition of a rule of law (for example, by a colonial power) or by an emergent nationalism.

The Furnivall plural-society approach at least makes it possible to overcome the first objection, since the dichotomy is not seen in extreme terms, and it becomes a matter of empirical investigation as to how much common interest there might be, and what the nature of the interaction (however minimal) across group boundaries might be.

This leads to the second objection, which is that it is not true that there is no interaction between the economies. The interaction indeed takes several highly significant forms, and it may be argued that if there are continuing differences in orientation, those differences themselves result from the interaction.

One such interaction was the force of competition itself, backed by political power which created powerful monopolies. There is ample evidence that Javanese, Macassarese, and other Indonesian traders were rich, active, and strong in the sixteenth and seventeenth centuries, and that no writer analyzing this period could accurately describe Indonesian society as being traditionally uninterested in commerce or in maximization. The wealth of the Indonesian ruling houses was indubitably based upon the vigorous commerce of their subjects, and the internal political rivalries of Indonesian groups, some of which continue in their effects even today, were linked with intrigues involving European commercial powers. Attempts to control these intrigues led not only to alterations in commercial balances within the archipelago, but also to monopoly by the Dutch, and the destruction of Indonesian commercial enterprise. It can be argued historically that the Dutch, by the force of their powerful competition and politically protected commerce, created the conditions under which a dual economy came to be.[9]

Under other conditions, such as those of Melanesia, the early establish-

[9] See, for example, B. Schrieke, *Indonesian Sociological Studies*, Part I (The Hague: Van Hoeve, 1955); J. C. von Leuw, *Indonesian Trade and Society* (The Hague: Van Hoeve, 1955); B. H. M. Vlekke, *Nusantara* (The Hague: Van Hoeve, 1959).

ment of a commercial role in the hands of a specific ethnic group creates an a priori advantage which, at a later stage, makes it difficult for the indigenous people to break into a particular field. Thus, for example, in the Solomon Islands, European planters and Chinese traders operated small trade stores, beginning at a time when commercial activity was well outside the ken of the indigenous people. Later this was thought of as something that Europeans and Chinese did, rather than natives, and a Solomon Islander breaking into the field would not only have to overcome this definition of ethnic role, but also to raise capital, learn commercial practice, and risk losing his whole enterprise by competing with already experienced and entrenched individuals.

Competition tended to favor the alien for other reasons. P. T. Bauer has pointed out that government services tended to help the entrenched planter rather than the peasant rubber tapper in Malaya, and the reasons for this suggest such a policy to be widespread, though without deliberate intent. The mode of operation of the commercial plantation is more readily understood by colonial officials and by research workers who share the value orientation of the planters. Sophisticated planters can exercise pressure for services more readily and know better what can be done. They are smaller in number and operate larger economic units than the peasants, are more readily accessible, the conditions of agriculture are more familiar to the research support, and they have more effective connections with international forces, including those who make the international agreements which often govern national policy (for example, international sugar production quotas).[10]

A related form of interaction is through competition for resources, particularly land and labor, since capital is almost exclusively available to the capitalist or modern sector. The success of the modern sector in acquiring land and labor is often of crucial importance in reducing the dynamic of the traditional economy. European plantation, farming, and mining interests have been exceedingly successful in obtaining title to resources under colonial conditions well before the indigenous population has been in a position to exploit them, despite genuine and far-reaching attempts by governments to restrict alien acquisition, particularly of land. In Kenya this was one of the most powerful factors keeping the sectors of the economy apart and preventing Africans from acquiring farming skills, since the African was relegated to overpopulated and less

---

[10] P. T. Bauer, *Report on a Visit to the Rubber-Growing Smallholdings of Malaya, July-September 1946*, Colonial Research Publications No. 1 (London: Colonial Office, 1948); *West African Trade* (London: Cambridge University Press, 1954); and P. T. Bauer and B. S. Yamey, *The Economics of Underdeveloped Countries* (Cambridge: Cambridge University Press, 1957).

fertile land.[11] Now that much of the better land has been opened up for African settlement, Africans have taken up farms and are endeavoring to acquire the skills so alien to their former way of life, with of course greatly varying success. Very rarely did colonial governments issue mining licenses to indigenous enterprises, since, among other things, in the name of technical and commercial efficiency they demanded a complex business and capital structure in the recipient of licenses.[12] The effect of land acquisition in such highly settled countries as the United States, Canada, Australia, New Zealand, and South Africa was traumatically to create dualism in the economy by debarring the indigenous inhabitants from creative participation in it for decades.

Competition for labor had perhaps less direct and more subtle effects. Western enterprise was able to offer exciting and effective inducements to many indigenous populations to offer their labor services. It is at this point, which is balanced by the supply of Western manufactured goods, that the notion of *independent* dual economies most completely breaks down, for this was the means by which a demand for money, and the things money could buy, gradually penetrated traditional economies, and this in turn led to attempts by the indigenous people from time to time to establish their own enterprises. The effects of migrant labor, whether as slave labor to create the new societies of the Caribbean, as mining labor to create the new towns of Africa and to alter profoundly the rural African way of life,[13] or as plantation labor introducing new ethnic groups into Malaya or Fiji or disrupting village society,[14] were among the most profound of those which resulted from European contact with privitive societies.

The drain of such labor supply frequently enervated rural society, and it was many years before it created a settled urban population from which new indigenous enterprise could spring. But the effects went further. The competition was for alternative uses for labor. An indigenous would-be entrepreneur had to ask himself whether he should spend his energies trying to compete by operating his own peasant plantation, or work for a wage. If he opted to work his own plantation, as many tried to do, he had to persuade rural villagers, already suffering through loss

[11] See *Report of the Kenya Land Commission, 1933* and *Report of the Royal Commission on East Africa, 1953-55* (London: Her Majesty's Stationery Office).

[12] For an example of indigenous enterprise battling such odds, and also for the limiting effect of land registration systems, see Cyril S. Belshaw, *Under the Ivi Tree* (London: Routledge & Kegan Paul, Ltd.; Berkeley: University of California Press, 1964).

[13] Audrey Richards, ed., *Economic Development and Tribal Change* (Cambridge, Heffer, n.d.).

[14] Cyril S. Belshaw, *Changing Melanesia* (Melbourne: Oxford University Press, 1954).

of manpower, to work for him instead of for the alternative plantation owner. In most cases he could depend only on kinship loyalties to secure his resources, since he lacked capital and a trade store and was not able to offer the excitement of travel to distant foreign parts and contact with urbanized people as an inducement.[15]

In some instances, however, competition for labor from the peasant sector was successful, and its very success often led to attack or at least suspicion by the advocates of the alien sector. The most dramatic instance of this was the success of the rubber small-holding in Malaya, despite the fact that it was ignored by government and in competition with highly capitalized plantations. Where peasant enterprise did compete in this way, it often showed more resilience than did the more capital-intensive sector, particularly in prewar conditions. The peasant could withdraw production in times of low prices, and often increase it heavily in times of high ones, by turning to subsistence as an alternative to cash earning, or by using forest resources to increase production, as the case might be. On the other hand, the plantation was forced to maintain a fairly steady rate of production to cover overheads or else close out altogether, while expansion was often a slow process involving planting new areas.

It is probably true that in areas such as Africa, Southeast Asia, and Oceania, the sophisticated economy failed to provide a working demonstration effect to stimulate the peasant economy. It was too readily possible for the indigenous population to account for the success of alien commercial methods by reference to a foreign cultural mystique, government favoritism, and similar psychological explanations. This sometimes led to movements of religious explanation, which competed directly with more secularly oriented enterprises, both political and economic.[16]

Two points emerge from this summary review. One is that many societies are imperfectly articulated, and that this imperfection operates to hold back the growth of the peasant or traditional sector. The other is that the various elements that make up plural societies are *in some form* of association and interaction, so that what happens in one sector affects to some degree the reactions of the other.

The first point is taken up by Albert O. Hirschman,[17] who argues that the flow of capital and enterprise in underdeveloped countries will be to

---

[15] W. E. Moore, *Industrialization and Labor* (Ithaca, N.Y.: Cornell University Press, 1951).

[16] Peter Worseley, *The Trumpet Shall Sound* (London: MacGibbon and Kee, 1957); and Vittorio Lanternari, *The Religions of the Oppressed* (New York: Alfred A. Knopf, Inc., 1963).

[17] Albert O. Hirschman, *The Strategy of Economic Development* (New Haven, Conn.: Yale University Press, 1958), pp. 125-32.

the highly capitalized sector of modern orientation, and that a very high proportion of creative energies will go to the establishment of new industry of this character, rather than to modernizing or changing technologically and commercially backward industries in the traditional sector. Dualism and the gap between the two sectors is likely to increase according to this analysis (until such time as the gap becomes politically untenable?).

The second point is that dualism or pluralism is not a phenomenon unique to colonial situations, but that it is a form of society exhibiting a variant on a theme present in all, namely social stratification. In a plural society the stratified groups are usually identifiable on ethnic grounds, but the relationships between the groups are of the same order as relationships between segments of other societies, though with differing weights and implications. There is thus much in common with a caste society, and something in common with a class society, in that the segments supplement one another, fulfill differentiated roles, and thus contribute to a division of labor necessary for exchange to take place. But caste and class societies, however much they may show signs of value differences as between their segments, operate to maintain an integrated system. In the plural society the integration is in process of being forged through the slow and painful creation of the institutions which will articulate it.

SIMILARITIES IN MODERN STATES

The examples we have given are of political economic units which, however much they may have served the needs of their time, do not meet contemporary criteria for viable, modern, and dynamic national economies. Of the examples, that of the dual economy has the most immediate and direct relevance for contemporary economic development, since for most of the world it represents the condition out of which contemporary modernization may emerge. Before considering the full requirements of modernization, it may be worthwhile to dwell on the features of these attempts at articulation which are present in contemporary economies.

In the first place, there is control over the economy exercised by a political authority. The philosophy and interests of such authorities are highly variable in the modern world, so that the objectives and the nature of the control vary considerably, and the economic system correlated with the political authority also varies. In particular, the systems examined in this chapter indicate the importance of the acts of the political authority in influencing the price system and in controlling international trade, two key areas of interest for all modern governments.

An approach to a price mechanism is not merely a technical economic matter, but must of necessity involve judgments about the validity of particular ways of distributing products and the desirability of the kinds of social relations which accompany the distributive process. This applies irrespective of particular philosophies about ownership of the means of production, since it is possible to have free ownership with administered prices (as in capitalist countries during war), or public ownership with free prices (although I know of no such case empirically, except in limited sectors of an economy, as with nationalized industries in Britain).

Nevertheless, two sharply differing approaches to prices are evident in capitalist and communist systems. In puristic terms, capitalist political economy implies that the state exerts its influence to create conditions under which prices find their own level through the interplay of market conditions related to competition and the exercise of financial, commercial, organizational, and productive power. Demand, expressed through the choices of purchasers (limited, however, to the goods presented to them), is one factor affecting prices, and supply the other. The philosophy of capitalism is often based upon the ethos of individual initiative and the merits of the system in rewarding efficiency and punishing inefficiency in the supply of the market.

We have noted, however, that conditions of pure competition are not profit making or capital accumulating; profits come to the entrepreneur who is quick off the mark, or who administers his affairs to create and maintain a position of advantage. Oligopolies and monopolies emerge from this situation, and are in some ways (despite tendencies towards bureaucratization) the most powerful elements in maintaining the dynamic of capitalism. But this runs counter to the ethos of individual opportunity and the increasing emphasis upon individual welfare. Hence capitalist states are increasingly intervening to modify the economic power structure, for example through control of key prices (as with some public utilities, or the prevention of price-fixing agreements among firms, or the enactment of minimum wage, that is labor-price, laws).

Communism, on the other hand, operates on the basis of administered prices. Such prices are fixed by institutions established by the state, and are part of a national plan which governs the direction and emphases of the total economy. Although fixed by regulation, the prices are not permanent but are modified from time to time to reflect changing conditions and objectives. Communist price fixing is by no means a denial of supply and demand, but a recognition of it, and a harnessing of it for state purposes. It is the state which sets the pattern of effective demand by setting prices which will make it easier or harder, as the case may be, for individuals to obtain the goods they want, creating shortages of goods the state does not want people to have.

Both capitalist and communist systems work at the level of supplying producers as well as consumers, so that these principles apply to the pricing of raw materials as well. When production is through public ownership, the communist factory must maintain complex monetary accounts and must balance its budget just as would a private firm. If the state decides that its product must be priced cheaply (for example, if cloth must be low in price in order to encourage the flow of cheap consumer clothing), the state must subsidize or recompense the factory, or the accounts will be out of balance and production threatened.

This is even clearer when we realize that the raw material (cotton, wool) comes from producers who, however organized, depend on the price for their personal incomes, and that the factory must be able to cover wages as well as buy materials from other state enterprises. On the one hand the state must try to keep the prices of finished products down where it wants a high rate of consumption, and it must keep wages and prices of raw materials high in order to encourage the productivity of labor. This it can do through taxation and by balancing profit-making industries against those where it is necessary to show a loss.

Ultimately, of course, the theory of communism implies a technological state in which there is plenty for all, scarcity is eliminated, and the state can distribute to all according to their need. But the realistic (theoretically transitional) state of communist socialism must recognize scarcity, as did ancient Babylonia, and administer prices with supply and demand in mind.

States emerging from colonial dualism have political decisions to make with regard to their pricing system. Indications are that there will be more direct political control of prices than was the case in capitalist societies in the early stages of their development, which took place in a laissez-faire era. In the first place, they are influenced by modern capitalism, which is more tolerant of price control, and which, in its colonial form, used authority to establish marketing boards and other institutions which governed prices, particularly of key export commodities. In addition, there is a strong ethical orientation towards "fair prices" and limiting fluctuations, particularly where fluctuations seem to be affected by market power operating outside the country itself. Finally, new nations are strongly committed to economic growth, and wish to use all the means in their power, including control over markets, to govern the factors which may contribute to economic growth.

As against these tendencies towards price and market control, we may note other factors which perpetuate elements of free marketing. The peasant is for price control when it is in his favor, but against it when he could obtain better conditions under free marketing and when controls appear to limit his action unduly. (The Ghana cocoa stabilization scheme has had political difficulties when world prices were too far above domestic prices.) Free marketing and bargaining have permeated the economies. And, perhaps most important in the short run, there are immense technical difficulties in establishing full planning in under-developed economies, where there is a great shortage of reliable statistics, of skilled bureaucrats, and of the finances to employ them. Even in the U.S.S.R. the extent of planning is limited by its practicability, and there are areas of free marketing where detailed control would just not be worthwhile. Such areas are much more extensive in nations poor in resources.

For these reasons, compromises between the two approaches to controls and pricing are to be expected, and possibly new solutions which may differ from those in capitalism or in communism strictly conceived.

Another theme which emerges from the examples is that boundaries of political significance come to have economic significance. The political authority, in modern terms the nation state, conceives of social relations within the state and between its nationals as being different from those external to the state and not fully subject to its authority. In part this is traceable to an ethic of nationality which implies differences between "we" and "they." In early Whydah and India the "they" were the foreign traders and merchants. In the colonial dual economy the "they" became incorporated in the state system as a superior layer in a hierarchy. In the new nations the "they" once again becomes the foreigner who operates with outside loyalties, the agents of capitalism or communism as they are seen to be. The political authority needs their services and must encourage them. At the same time it must protect itself from those actions which may threaten its independence, organic integrity, and long-run objectives. The foreigner must commit himself completely to the objectives of the new nation or must fit into one of the new roles being defined and prepared for him.

The technical actions of new nations in this field consist largely of control over investment and imports and exports. There may be, for example, encouragement of investment by tax relief, but at the same time an insistence upon some form of partnership with indigenous interests. In an endeavor to retain purchasing power within the nation and to encourage investment in local production there are often quotas or penal taxes on imports not regarded as essential to the economy, thus preventing consumers from spending on imports to the detriment of the flow of, for example, industrial machinery. This again was a problem faced by the early ports of trade. However, in modern times it is resorted to by many economies which are wrestling with balance-of-trade problems. New Zealand, for example, for a long time had extremely restrictive policies with regard to the movement of capital and imports.

Such measures imply notions not merely of political in-groups and out-groups, but also the idea that the political boundary encloses an economy which in some real sense is a viable system. New nations are desperately endeavoring to give meaning to this ideal and to translate it into reality. In the next chapter we shall examine in more detail what the requirements are for a viable modern economy. It will be evident that almost all political units, however drawn, could achieve some such state, but that given existing political boundaries it is not necessarily the most effective or productive policy. There are perhaps some conditions (size, balance of resources, availability of personnel) which are ideal for the operation of an economic system, and others under which the costs and difficulties of setting one up are expensive and inefficient. Should political boundaries be re-drawn to encompass viable economies? Is it possible to have differing boundaries for effective political and economic systems? These are practical issues as well as theoretical ones. They are among the issues, for example, which lie behind the controversy over whether Europe can be a single economy with independent states in partnership, and whether the economic dependence of Canada upon the United States means Canada's political extinction.

The third theme emerging from the examples is that of social stratification and the assignment of roles in the economic system. The port of trade and Babylonian examples give an indication of the role of the bureaucrat in determining relations between merchants and in engaging in trade directly as state mercantile entrepreneurs. This is a role carrying with it power and status implications which we must examine again in the context of modernization, since it is of great significance in socialist countries, and in those new nations where state or cooperative ventures are being established to fill gaps left by private enterprise. In the latter context, however, the bureaucratic intervention is less in trade itself than in production.

The colonial dual economy example is, as we have indicated, one of stratification linked with ethnic distinctions and specialization of role. Stratification in capitalist class societies is of a different order from that of plural societies in that (1) there is no ethnic correlation with class, and (2) class groups are not always identifiable in a sense that indicates group solidarity and organization, endogamy, lack of mobility across boundaries, and so forth, as is the case with, for example, the Europeans of colonial society. This having been said, it still remains to point out that modern capitalist societies and the new nations show a wide diversity of stratification and of economic correlates. It could be argued that the bureaucracy and the managerial elite in Western societies, including those of the communist world, are differentiated sharply from the rest of society both as to their role and function and as to their education, values, and outlook. The recruitment into such groups is vastly different from recruitment into components of a plural society, and there are different qualities of relationships as the groups interact. But any analysis of operating social structure must take into account the differentiation of such groups, their special role in the division of labor, and the nature of interaction, just as was the case when we examined plural societies.

A further point should be noticed. When we talk of stratification we are inclined to think of horizontal ranks ordered in a hierarchy, and we speak of class when there is some mobility and caste when there is practically none. But vertical segmentation is very similar to horizontal stratification and carries with it significant implications for exchange and the economic system. It is, of course, a commonplace in anthropology that vertically segmented lineages can be hierarchically ranked, and the rank can be based upon an ethos, as in Fiji, which ascribes to each lineage a specialized function, such as that of priests, warriors, fishermen, and the like. One only has to give reality to these functions and convert the lineages into endogamous units instead of exogamous ones, and there exists a caste system. In many societies, however, the functions are symbolic rather than real, the lineages are exogamous, and exchange is not of specialties but of goods and services of a like kind.

In complex societies the same kind of approach to segmentation leads to similar results. In a plural society the elements are hierarchically arranged. But in the early history of the formation of nations, and in the contemporary history of nation building, the polity frequently contains within it parallel segments, ethnically identified, and with differentiated economic functions, some of which carry status implications. It was the case in Canada for many years, for example, that French Quebec, structurally parallel to the English-speaking provinces, was differentiated not only in language and culture but in economic role. The productive and technical backwardness of Quebec, coupled with inadequate control of her political destiny, carried status implications. There is now, of course, considerable agitation to improve status, but not so much to remove the parallel association.

In Europe the formation of national states often came about through the painful association of parallel segments, each with a dialectical difference and sometimes a specialized economic position, ruled sometimes by the domination of one group, and ultimately leading to a much greater degree of fusion. In Africa, India, and the new states of Southeast Asia parallelism is of just as much importance as pluralism, since in many instances the ethnic components are differentiated regionally and economically, have differing ethical systems, and have different technical and educational resources upon which to base their organization and economic growth. Such countries are often politically organized on a federated basis and have special problems in securing a viable articulation of their economy, which by and large, have not been examined as special economic phenomena.

The economic systems we have described, with the exception of the Babylonian, have immediate relevance for the modern world, since they typify conditions out of which the modernization of new nations is taking place. The task of such nations is to convert their economies into modern viable units which will be a bulwark in the construction of independence, which will satisfy the aspirations of their peoples, which will make it possible to live securely alongside their neighbors, and which will in most cases provide a dynamic that will enable the nation to keep pace with world developments. Furthermore, many nations (India, China, Venezuela, Egypt) which have modern industrial sectors also contain populations that subscribe to a way of life similar to that indicated previously, with which any country must eventually have to come to terms, or change radically. The movement we are witnessing is immense, since such economies must not only catch up to the present but also move faster than advanced countries if they are to maintain their position. Already there are signs that despite vigorous and unprecedented change in the last two decades, the gap between the rich and the poor nations is increasing because of the great speed of development in industrial countries, and because of the concentration of capital, skills, and organization in them. Here we must focus upon one aspect, complex enough, of this phenomenon. What

CHAPTER FIVE

Conditions for the Modernization
of the Market Economy

are the necessary conditions for the conversion of societies into modern economies? I will not argue that such conversion is inevitable, automatic, or historically predictable. This is a separate question to which some answers are possible, lying in the field of culture change theory. What I am asking, rather, is this: Insofar as nations or societies can control their destiny rationally, what are the principles which they must bear in mind if they are to achieve a modernization of their market system?

We must first set aside one group of myths which can bedevil the analysis. The societies we have been considering are certainly very different from the modern complex bureaucracies and economies of Western capitalism and the communist world. But the differences lie in the scale, the complexity, and the ramifications of the systems, not in fundamental attributes of human nature. While it is true that some societies may be characterized by fatalism and inaction, this should not be thought of as a basic premise of the society in question, but as an element in a complex of conditions which are subject to change. It is possible to set up a personality or character profile for a society, but this in itself says nothing about the endurance and permanence of the traits listed under varying conditions of pressure.

Furthermore the overwhelming majority of societies are achievement oriented, even where roles are heavily ascribed, and the maximization of satisfaction principle is at work in all of them. What differs, as we have noted before, is the legitimate field of achievement and the factual manifestation of satisfaction. Societies reward different acts in different ways, but reward something they always do; and men differ in their wants.

In addition, men in all societies must organize their resources and take risks in doing so: the entrepreneurial function is omnipresent and a condition of any form of social life. Any form of organization of resources involves the expenditure of time, and this cannot be done without some minimal form of planning or thinking ahead. All societies go beyond the minimal planning and seek to improve their level of living through capital investment. Man, it is said, is a toolmaker. This, the most elementary first element in culture, perhaps predating language, offers the evolutionist the first glimmerings of the emergence of humankind. Yet to create tools is to invest capital, for this act uses resources (including time and labor) now in order to provide a durable and more complex resource for future production. All human societies are societies of capital investors.

Achievement orientation, maximization, enterprise, and capital investment are not, therefore, characteristics which have to be created *de novo,* although many theories of economic growth in underdeveloped countries naively assume the contrary, and base their arguments upon it. The task of modernization is rather to harness these principles to a new institutional complex, and to put them to work in an altered context.

THE BASIS OF EXCHANGE

The exchange system of all economies, whether modern or not, derives from two sets of conditions. On the demand side, there are, at the moment of individual actions, specific unsatiated wants which define the goals of activity. If wants are limited in range, are so patterned that they are unchanging over long periods, and are satisfied in a high proportion of instances by direct action on the part of the person in need, the economy is simple. By contrast, modern economies are characterized by a great variety of wants which tend to expand as fast as the facilities to satisfy them. The achievement of each level of satisfaction, whether of individuals or of the society at large, opens the way to a new range of demand; the threshold of satisfaction is continually changing. The patterns of demand vary according to population groups within the society, differentiated on ethnic, class, income, educational, and other lines. The time over which a particular pattern continues to have validity can seldom be predicted with certainty. All economies are based on unsatiated objectives, but a modern economy does not expect to reach a static equilibrium between demand and supply which is typical of most primitive societies.

On the supply side, all exchange is based on differentiation of role. If this were not the case, we would have islands of individuals engaged in a Robinson Crusoe self-sufficient economy. In some primitive societies, it is true, the differentiation is linked primarily with membership in a particular lineage, the individuals concerned having command over much the same kind of resources as their neighbors. This leads to circulating prestatory exchange of the same kinds of goods. But in most societies the differentiation goes further, so that different individuals, groups, or corporate institutions command different kinds of resources and combine them to produce a variety of goods. In modern societies such differentiation is highly complex.

Differentiation of role is closely linked with the scarcity factor, which is a major element in economic theory. Each role implies that the persons ascribed to it have the right to control defined resources and use them in defined and approved ways. This in turn implies the right to exclude others from the resources and actions, or to secure cooperation as the case may be. The distribution of property rights is thus a fundamental datum governing the pattern of social roles, and is the primary element in the definition of scarcity in a given society.

The action correlate of differentiated roles is division of labor, which of course is based not only on the way property is controlled, but also on the distribution of skills and socially approved behavior. Unsatiated wants and division of labor create exchange.

Again, modern economies are characterized by a high degree of division of labor. This is an essential part of the modern system of exchange, since division of labor makes it possible to use technical specialization with greatest efficiency. It also makes it possible for a flow of wealth to take place, leading to profit-taking situations and the ability to accumulate capital. There are, however, technical and organizational conditions which place a limit on the effective division of labor in any given society, thus limiting its capacity to achieve a more complex socioeconomic structure.

COORDINATING MECHANISMS

All economies have coordinating mechanisms, but the complexities of modern societies require that these have special orientations and elaborations, if the economy is to be viable.

At this point one should introduce an important qualification into the analysis. It may appear that I am arguing that if certain conditions are not present, the society cannot be viable, or at least cannot be modern. The fact of the matter is that no society is without stress, strain, distortion, imperfection; if man were completely rational, God-like, and in control, he could improve the operations of any society. The point is not whether a given society is completely efficient and perfect, but to what degree it has been able to achieve its goals, the degree to which its institutions contribute to them, and how it compares with other societies in these matters. Of these points, the last is the most value free and objective. What we shall be setting out here are not criteria of perfection, but criteria against which the nature and performance of a society might be judged, within the context of a market economy.

Value Orientations

It is a truism of sociology and anthropology that value orientations define the scope and range of social action, and are indeed a primary dimension in culture. The complexities which lie behind this statement [1]

[1] For a viewpoint on these, together with bibliographical references to such writers as Clyde Kluckhohn and Morris Opler, see Cyril S. Belshaw, "The Identification of Values in Anthropology," *American Journal of Sociology,* 64, No. 6 (1959), 555-62; and "Social Structure and Cultural Values as Related to Economic Growth," *International Social Science Journal,* 26, No. 2 (1964), 189-96.

cannot be expanded upon here, but some clarification is necessary.

Value orientations are not values, but are the principles which can be discerned as underlying the formation and selection of values. Values themselves are wants or goals weighted according to the force with which they govern action, bearing in mind their positive desirability and the negative costs which must be paid to achieve them. At any given time, there are two categories of values, namely those which govern actual specific action, thus forming an observed pattern of behavior or a demand schedule, and those which are present in men's minds as ultimate objectives, ethical principles, and the like, which *might* govern specific action if opportunities and costs were to change. Such hopes and ambitions constitute the economist's potential demand.

We think of cultures as entities because patterns and unifying principles link values and provide value orientations. The processes which create value orientations are thus unifying and coordinating mechanisms for social action, including the economy, and value orientations once formed give a circumscribing framework to future action. The ethos of a culture consists of the normative principles which describe proper conduct, some of which may be translated into rules or laws. World view, cosmology, philosophy, provide the ideas within which men view their environment, predict its behavior, and therefore on which they base their actions. Mythology links these principles together and gives both an explanation for the world and society and a manipulable set of case histories upon which to base a justification for behavior. Processes of socialization, and in the modern world the pressures of communication, form men's minds, shaping them into the particular set of value orientations valid for a given culture.

These forces are present in all cultures, but do they have any special relevance for the modern market economy? Without them, the modern economy could probably not exist, for upon consistency in such patterns psychological prediction is based, at least in the lay world. The businessman's confidence leans heavily upon his knowledge of his competitor's and supplier's behavior, which in turn is formed by his knowledge of patterned behavior in the culture. It also leans upon his knowledge of his legal and contractual rights, which are the more formalized elements of the pattern, supported by the political and judicial institutions.

But does not the market economy depend for its strength and adaptability upon the untrammeled play of competitive individual interest? It might be possible to construct a society on such a basis, if everyone subscribed to the ethic, and if each individual expected every other to act accordingly. But unrestricted individual competition is neither a *necessary* condition of modernity, nor an operative one in its extreme form. The functional success of socialism in some communist countries shows it not to be necessary, but even in Western capitalism the assertion has the status of mythology rather than reality. It is the principle against which action is justified when called in question. But in fact individual interest is formed and controlled in a vast number of ways, by the creation of values in the home and in society, by the self-interest of individuals which leads them to compromise with groups, and by the institutions of the state.

Furthermore, most individuals in modern just as in peasant society flee from the insecurity of fresh decision making. While some are innovators, and while innovation is praised and rewarded, even innovation is easier when it is patterned. But most decision makers are not innovators: they are men who make routine decisions according to precedent. The small shopkeeper does not normally seek maximum profit to find what the traffic will bear, and if he varies his prices according to the bargaining power of his customer he will be accused of every nefarious chicanery. Instead, he works to a percentage markup. Similarly, the executive in a large corporation works to precedent: if he has a new idea, he must "sell" it to committees and to those higher in authority by techniques which are as often as not those of psychological power plays rather than the cold detached appraisal of technical effectiveness.[2]

Patterning, then, is indubitably a foundation of modern economies, and it does not have to be of the individualistic pure competition kind. But does it have to be just one pattern in any given society?

This is a question that needs much more investigation. The national character anthropologists such as Margaret Mead and Geoffrey Gorer have tended to stress the uniformities in cultural patterns in complex societies, and even the permanence of the basic traits underlying them. The methodology and conclusions of such approaches are highly dubious, and even if truth be hidden in them we must still face the fact that in complex societies such as the United States, the U.S.S.R., France, Britain, and Canada, there are considerable differences in point of view between large sections of the population. Admittedly, differences in point of view may cover greater uniformities in behavior than would appear on first sight. Again, a differentiated role system may allocate persons who have appropriate views to appropriate roles. The technical innovator may become the plant engineer, the routine-minded bureaucrat the accountant, the extrovert the salesman, and so on. Thus a complex society can accommodate itself and perhaps even take advantage of differences of viewpoint.

One might also argue that if a modern society is to be dynamically

---

[2] See the pioneering study, not adequately followed up by others, by George Katona, *The Psychological Analysis of Economic Behavior* (New York: McGraw-Hill Book Company, 1951).

oriented it must accommodate and make use of diversity in value orientation. Innovation consists in the rearrangement of old ideas and components of knowledge more than it does in pure discovery. The more a society is diversified, the more rapid its rate of innovation.

It is also necessary to recognize that value orientations, even in modern societies, are not normally universalistic in the Parsonian sense. True, there are important sectors in which men make decisions on the basis of technical factors alone, and especially on price, supply, and demand alone. The stock market is the prime example, and so is the awarding of contracts on the basis of competitive tender. But in most transaction links there is a blend of particularism and universalism. Relatives or friends of owners of a business firm have entree when it comes to employment. A department store manager uses credit to bind his customers to him. A housewife, having established a link with a supermarket, knows what to expect there, chats with the girl at the check-out counter, and thenceforth limits her shopping around for competitive bargains. In analyzing such behavior, it is better to avoid tagging it as based on either universalistic or particularistic premises, but to ask, for example, at what point do considerations of advantage outweigh particularistic connections in influencing a change of behavior?

The Allocative and Distributive System

Whereas the value orientation system governs goals and modes of behavior, the allocative system associated with it distributes resources, both within the productive process, and through the exchange which links producers and consumers. Modern societies blend the direct allocation of resources by political authority and the acquisition of resources freely through the use of a medium of exchange.

It cannot be taken for granted that a medium of exchange circulates through all significant transactions in an underdeveloped economy, but in a modern one both private and state transactions depend upon it. States do not have the techniques for the deliberate manipulation of prestatory systems, but they can readily interfere with monetary systems. We have already noted that they can (within limits) control prices.

In addition, they can tax personal income and use the proceeds to provide grants and welfare payments which are essentially means of redistributing purchasing power. Personal taxation is well-nigh impossible in a complex state without a monetary means of exchange. Taxes levied on corporations or other productive units can be either a monetary accounting procedure, or, as in the U.S.S.R., the allocation of some proportion of production to the state pool of resources. This can then be distributed by sale, or by direct allocation.

It should also be noted that in some countries (for example, the United States and Canada) well-organized public pressure supplements income redistribution. Campaigns for charitable purposes and the power organization of community chests, ramifying through the social and economic structure, are cases in point.

Again, the state can acquire resources on its own account by declaring them to be its property (in the case, for example, of undiscovered minerals), by expropriation, or by purchase, and can then use these powers to create productive units under its direct control, or can allocate them by sale or license to private users. Fundamentally, all property in complex societies depends upon its recognition as such by the state, whether derived from traditional experience, as in Europe or Africa, or from the historical exercise of colonizing powers, as in North America. In America the states protected, defined, and legitimized the acquisition of property by colonists, and this distribution was the foundation for subsequent productive enterprise (plus, of course, the immigration of labor and capital resources from older countries).

The action or inaction of the state is then an essential element in the distributive system. But apart from that, income depends upon the resources controlled, the manner in which they are combined to create a product, and the price purchasers are prepared to pay for it. The ability of producers and suppliers to match returns and costs governs their ability to continue in operation, although that ability may well be affected by state intervention (subsidy, punitive taxation). The extension of this feature throughout the economy is essential to modernity. Unless the allocation and distributive system coordinates all major sectors of the economy, we cannot speak of a unified modern economy. This matter is intimately linked with adjustive mechanisms.

The Entrepreneur

A key figure in coordination is the entrepreneur. This is a very loose term indicating a variety of functions, some of which may be combined in one role or distributed through a number.

In one sense, an entrepreneur is simply a combiner of resources, that is, a production manager whose task it is to decide how much of what kinds of capital, labor, and raw materials are to be combined and in what ways they are to be organized. This is the act of making economizing decisions (in production rather than consumption), and is very commonly distributed. Indeed, wherever there is an organization, there is an entrepreneurial-management function, even though it may be vested in a committee or a bureaucrat.

But this kind of management (as distinct from the day-to-day technical administration of production routines) involves risks, because judgments may be incorrect, and because at this level there are direct financial implications. The entrepreneur is taking risks in order to gain a profit; these are measured in monetary terms. In older economics, this element of risk taking was sharply focused, because it was assumed that the entrepreneur was working with his own money or resources, or that he was so close to ownership that profit or loss affected him personally.

It is difficult nowadays to sort out the function of risk taking in quite the same way. Managers of state corporations are using public property: the public gains the benefit of efficient administration and correct adventurous judgment, and loses if opposite conditions apply. The relationship is similar in the case of large joint stock companies, except that, in addition to salary, the decision maker may be rewarded by company stock, and thus shares directly in its fortunes. Nevertheless, the directors of such companies are essentially acting in trust for other owners, just as are directors of public corporations.

In essence, the function of risk taking becomes the function of committing an organization to a path of action based upon seizing an advantage which shows promise of placing that organization in a better position in the future. It is an adventurous act which has expansion as its orientation. Furthermore, it may even aim at the *reduction of risks* by eliminating a competitor, gaining control over resources, or establishing a lasting exchange relationship.

Sociologically speaking, then, risk taking is not a good way of characterizing one of the entrepreneurial functions. That function is better thought of as a propensity to take advantage of opportunities with an orientation toward expansion.

This is very close to a third function which has been emphasized more and more in the economic literature, namely that of innovating. This idea too needs close sociological examination. A social or cultural innovation means the creation of some new kind of material artifact, mode of behavior, or idea, and its adoption by enough persons or with enough force to be a significant part of the social order and with some permanence. It is not merely an idiosyncrasy. An innovator is not necessarily a manager of a productive enterprise, but may be an employee or someone quite outside it. Entrepreneurs who innovate *from the point of view of their own firm* are quite common; they simply make changes. Entrepreneurs who innovate *from the point of view of the economy* are much rarer. Copying from others, that is, adopting or spreading an innovation, is probably statistically much commoner in complex societies than the original act of innovation itself.

Nevertheless, one thing is clear. Modern economies are characterized by a comparatively widespread distribution of enterprise in its various forms, as opportunity seizing, as innovating, and as innovation spreading. This applies in public as well as in private sectors.

Legitimate Authority

All the themes so far treated in this chapter come together when we make the statement that modern economic coordination depends upon the legitimate exercise of authority without which decision making cannot be effective, whether it be at the familial, the organizational, or the state level.

It will be noted that no prior assumption has been made about the location or distribution of this authority, nor as to whether it must be based upon rationalized or charismatic loyalties. The effectiveness of different types of authority may one day be compared in this context, but at the moment we can only note that the value orientations of different cultures reward and legitimize quite different authority patterns in differing institutional contexts, apparently with comparable effectiveness. Authority in the Japanese family firm, quite successful in building up gigantic mercantile empires, differed in important ways from that typical of the Lancashire cotton miller, the Rothschilds, the Soviet bureaucratic manager, and the organization man of a United States corporation. But in each case the authority was legitimized, that is, it was recognized as being properly exercised; it stimulated effective responses within the organization; and it was located in the organization in a manner consonant with the country's ethos, or that of an influential group within it.

The Bureaucracy

Modern bureaucracies always have some important influence on the private sector of activity. Insofar as exchange is concerned, the question is, to what degree do they exercise their influence deliberately, and, insofar as they do, is this effective? Do they, in other words, succeed in what they are trying to do?

Whether they plan with communist totality, or whether they restrict themselves to a small but influential aspect of activity (for example, manipulating interest and exchange rates), bureaucracies must base deliberate acts on information and its analysis. It is probably true to say that the relationship between government and the economy is closer today than, let us say, in eighteenth-century Europe, simply because bureaucratic technology and information analysis is more sophisticated. It is now, for example, possible to design and administer a direct tax to achieve a given result much more effectively than it was eighty years ago.

The ability of a bureaucracy to influence the speed and direction of economic change is thus very great, but it is dependent upon the existence of certain conditions. Among these are the analytic skill and training of the civil servants, the degree to which they are influenced by a priori notions or ineffective theories, and the ability to gather meaningful information by statistical and other means. Information gathering is a costly and sophisticated process which is not always within the means of countries trying to modernize fast. In some instances, important sectors are not clearly or directly related to monetary measurement, either because exchange is nonmonetary, or because qualitative, nonmeasurable data are all important. Thus, for example, it is one thing to measure the cost of education, but quite another to indicate a relationship between cost and quality.

Nevertheless, there is a relationship between the speed of modernization and the effectiveness of bureaucratic analysis and action.

Political Articulation

The political system is significant to economic modernization both because it can assist in the process and because its deficiencies can create insecurity or an inhospitable social environment.

For the political structure to be effectively articulated, its different elements must be in a stimulating relationship. This applies, for example, to the relationship between civil servant and politician, particularly if the former is a diagnostician and analyst as well as an executive official. The adjustment of government departments one to another is sometimes achieved outside the formal lines of communication through personal transactions of an informal character between civil servants, the relationships being founded on such matters as common goals, friendships, and shared sociopolitical backgrounds.

Controlled articulation also frequently involves independent, quasi-independent, or controlled organizations which have a public character. Cooperatives in many new countries are regulated by a specific government department which has an intimate involvement in their affairs, and in others federations of cooperatives may have sufficient strength to influence political action. Similar remarks apply to trade unions and charitable organizations.

It also applies, in a more complicated way, to relationships between different levels and departments of government. This is a matter of obvious concern where government takes a primary initiative in managing an economy, as in communist systems, where a congruity of decision

making must be established between central, regional, and local governments, and between these and state-owned enterprises. In democratic
capitalist countries, the problem of coordination, division of responsibility, and delegation of authority is still present with a marked influence
on the pattern of the economy.

The interplay is recognized through such devices as central financial
aid for the redevelopment of blighted cities, this in turn involving city
government and a quasi-independent redevelopment agency. Other examples include the relationship between central government, local authority, and voluntary community chest agencies for the distribution of
welfare funds which, as we have seen, is part of the process of re-
allocating resources; and the establishment of regional land-use authorities or multipurpose development organizations such as the Tennessee
Valley Authority, all of which have an impact on the production and
exchange of goods and services and all of which involve complex inter-
agency relationships.

A new nation seeking modernity has a special problem to face. The
civil service ethos which it inherits may, as in British colonies, have
been against local governments taking direct responsibility for productive or commercial enterprises. But the availability of managerial skills
can be in such short supply, and the necessity for coordination so urgent,
that no economic development will take place in the areas outside the
metropolis if left to private initiative. Local or regional authorities using
public resources must therefore not only build roads to the strategic
locations, but also found production and marketing cooperatives, create
a credit supply, operate bus and trucking lines, and engage in marketing.
In doing so, such authorities must respond to the policy of the central
government and work to some degree as its agent. But at the same time,
since public opinion is often lacking in an organized form, local authorities represent public opinion and are therefore obliged to inform central
government of local potentialities and conditions, to resist schemes which
are impractical or not wanted, and to suggest positive initiatives.

Since private enterprise in newly developing nations is often weak
from the point of view of mobilizing large-scale resources, or distributing
resources and initiatives throughout the country, a heavy responsibility
rests with all organs of government. It might indeed be said that a
sensitive and effective political apparatus which takes responsibility for
economic change at all levels constitutes the main element in the economic system of newly developing countries. Yet it is of necessity imperfectly achieved, creates heavy demands on skills, and its lack can
be a major obstacle in the path of modernization.

ADJUSTMENT REACTION SYSTEMS

The coordination systems referred to above are a special form of interaction in which conscious decisions are taken to achieve an approximate unity of purpose, and to move various elements in the economy toward a goal. But in studying the articulation of the economy, it is important to ask how and by what means the elements in the system react to one another. One firm, for example, is another's environment. If firm A changes its behavior, how does firm B respond? And what are the ultimate effects of these patterns of reaction on the economy as a whole?

There is, of course, no strict line between coordination and adjustment reaction. For example, in political coordination an element contributing to success is the feedback of knowledge, information and ideas from the local to the central government. If the central government exerts its authority without being sensitive to feedback, it is more than likely that its policies will encounter critical resistance or be impractical. Political parties help to provide feedback, but the direct reaction responsibility of local governments is always important, and more important in countries where political parties are themselves having problems of identification with the people.

Reactive Aspects of the Market

A major characteristic of the complex modern market is the widespread use of money as an accounting and exchange unit. Like that of other weights and measures, the value of money is subject to arbitrary authority and can be standardized by government. Such standardization is usually in terms of one or more specific equivalents, gold for example, or another foreign currency. But unlike other measures, the value of money is deliberately changed when government deems it appropriate (for example, devaluation), and it also changes in terms of specific commodities according to forces which may have nothing to do with the physical attributes of those commodities. The forces consist of the subjective judgments of buyers and sellers. It is as if a tree were ten feet or twelve feet high according to the subjective judgment of people who photographed it. The value of money is a social phenomenon, reacting to and upon social forces.

All commodities in any economy have real prices. That is, one may compute their costs of production, or may observe how much of another commodity they are exchanged for. In most economies, such prices are linked to form a consistent system. In monetary ones, the system is achieved through the common use of money as both exchange and accounting unit. In a modern economy all commodities and services except some of those provided within the family or transferred as gifts are accounted for in terms of money.

For newly developing nations, there are several implications of this familiar point. One is that, to achieve modernity, monetary accounting must penetrate the subsistence sector, linking it with the commercial sector, and providing a reaction mechanism between them. This would make it possible, for example, for a subsistence farmer to calculate what the costs of subsistence farming are by comparison with the costs and returns of market farming. By and large this is achieved, not by complex bookkeeping, but when all the factors used in subsistence farming also enter commercial exchange and are known to have a price there.

This leads to the second implication, which is that all utilizable resources should be available for pricing and open to buying and selling. There should be a market for land, for labor,[3] and for capital. Yet the entry of each of these all-important factors into the market may be quite foreign to the traditional exchange system of new nations. The limitation of monetized exchange to commodities already produced will place a barrier in the reactive system.

The utility of money is greater and its flow easier the more it is recognized to be part of a symbolic accounting system, rather than a physical commodity. The movement of millions of dollars in large physical transactions would clearly be an impossible friction in today's commercial world. Today's peasants, entering the commercial world at the opposite extreme of scale, must learn the techniques of monetary symbol language if they are to communicate with reactive sensitivity in a modern economy, yet by and large few institutions, except the school of inadequate experience, are available to teach them the conventions of accounting, credit, and banking.

The flow of money, of commodities, and the interlinkage of prices comes about because what is a finished product of no further direct use to one man is a needed commodity as a resource for further production or as a consumption good to another, because money is used to account for the transaction, and because transactions are compared. There is a continuous search for more economical and more secure terms of trade. The buying and selling actions of one man or firm are a part of the environment of others, which they must take into account.

A man or organization uses monetary devices to calculate the desir-

[3] See particularly W. E. Moore and A. S. Feldman, *Labor Commitment and Social Change in Developing Areas* (New York: Social Science Research Council, 1960).

ability of different courses of reaction to his environment, whether it be stabilized or changing. He makes judgments about the profitability and monetary implications of opportunities which are presented by the actions or inactions of others, by knowledge about what they are prepared to buy, about what others are producing, about commodities which are not being produced in adequate quantity, and so forth. Similarly, his judgment is affected by his knowledge of costs, expressed primarily in monetary terms, although affected by other considerations, such as the psychological costs of changing one's mode of life. In this sense, the market is an environment which provides opportunities, costs, and information enabling producers and consumers to react.

Reactions are not merely decisions to buy and sell, but also to establish an enterprise or direct it into appropriate channels. Economists draw attention to two types of reactive linkage.[4] Backward linkage exists when an enterprise requires products or services which are lacking and calls them into being. Forward linkage exists when an enterprise produces goods and services which then become the foundation for new activities. Such linkages clearly depend, not only on an integrated pricing system, but on the existence of a class of entrepreneurs who are knowledgeable about opportunities and who are in a position to exploit them.

Reactive responses of the kind indicated here take place between units of action such as individuals and organizations. The fact that such units may be independently controlled and owned is in some ways incidental. Large corporations must provide for reactive links of the same kind by dividing responsibility into action units and by accounting for inputs and outputs between them. The techniques are not very different from those which would exist between independent units, except that negotiation and bargaining take place in a committee room subject to ultimate authority instead of being based upon free pressures.

Mobility of Production Factors

A major feature of modern market economies is that those who control the factors of production are able to move them from one use to another as technical and economic conditions change; the factors are mobile as between uses. In addition, while it is true that there are many frictions of movement, factors can move from one owner to another, if the new owner is prepared to pay the price.

It should not be assumed that traditional economies lack such mobilities within their own systems. Land use and transfer, for example, was often highly mobile when political and lineage interests

[4] A. O. Hirschman, *The Strategy of Economic Development* (New Haven, Conn.: Yale University Press, 1958), Chap. 6.

exerted pressures. But the need for mobility in traditional societies is relatively restricted, and the conventions did not correspond with those applied by colonial agents of law and order. Thus it was typically the case that land registration systems, or systems of land reservation, restricted mobility.

Restrictions on mobility are often a major factor holding back the advance to modernity, and yet unrestricted mobility might create such insecurity and concentration of resources in few hands as to hold back the advance in other ways. It is not possible to review the institutional attempts to resolve this dilemma, imperfect as most of them are, but the essential conditions of mobility must be set out.

One is that land and natural resources should reach the hands of the most effective producers. Traditional societies, faced with fears of insecurity, are often extremely reluctant to change their patterns of land holding. For one thing, such change may involve migration, the acceptance of strangers into villages, and movement from tried small-scale techniques to unknown large-scale ones. But there is little reason to believe that a man born in a village oriented to traditional agriculture is necessarily a better *modern* agriculturalist than a man born in a fishing community. Yet every pressure can operate to prevent a man from moving from a community where one occupation is stressed to another with a different occupational emphasis, unless he moves to a city. Mobility of landholders in rural areas is sometimes nil. Clearly, mobility in the ownership and use of basic resources is closely bound up with mobility, or its lack, in occupations.

This matter is also linked with the ways in which a society recruits persons to occupational roles. It is emphatically not normal to find individuals in a society choosing of their own free will and without pressure to fill the needed positions. The role structure of a society, and hence its division of labor, is a resultant of past history and experience, and builds in a complex way upon the known skills and occupational interests of its population, combining these into a functional system. But the known skills and interests are themselves brought into being by the system of rewards and punishments that is in effect and the opportunities that have existed, and by the internalization over time of the habitual actions and valuations which are appropriate to slowly evolving conditions. By 1939 the occupational role of airline pilot was only just becoming systematized, with its own line of preliminary training and experience, with knowledge upon which to predict success and failure, and with its predictable rewards and costs. Few at that time would have predicted that in 1965 the role of computer programmer would be established and that of astronaut would be in the making.

Modern economy requires a great flexibility in role patterns and a system of rewards, sanctions, and recruitment which will ensure that roles are filled as needed. New nations have some advantages in this respect, but they also have critical disadvantages. At a certain level of technology, unskilled labor, of which most such countries have a surplus, is highly mobile and can be assigned to numerous roles as the occasion demands. At a very high level of technology, many skills of specific kinds are interchangeable among a number of production tasks, for the mode of analysis or action is abstract and generalized, just as mathematics is applicable to a wide variety of contents. Managers, computer programmers, sales staff, are often equally competent if switched from one product to another, or even one industry to another.

It follows that if new nations wish to modernize fast, to move flexibly, they will need to obtain men and women who can operate at a high level of generality and interchangeability. Since they will be creating many industries for the first time, they can take full advantage of automated processes which call for fewer persons of higher skills; and, provided costs are not too great, their newly educated technological elite can obtain the kind of new education which fits the processes well. Far from sneering at the application of computers and automation in newly developing countries, one should recognize that this may be a means to their industrial revolution and the way in which they can catch up to the West.

But between these two highly generalized types of labor lie a vast range of tasks for which specific training to a specific job is necessary, sometimes at very great length. Similarly, there is sometimes a status structure of roles which is not appropriate to the requirements of the market economy (an overproduction of classical scholars or lawyers, for example) or the structure appropriate at one time does not alter in order to enable the economy to meet new social and economic requirements (some analysts describe Latin America in this way). Both conditions limit mobility of occupational roles.

It should here be mentioned that formal education plays a large part in forming expectations about occupations and in creating or preventing a potential for mobility. This is dramatized by the experience of some international aid programs. Practical down-to-earth advice is necessary, but this implies an ability of the foreign aid expert to break out of his own cultural boundaries and to innovate in terms of the requirements of the society he is helping. Perhaps the majority of experts have been men who have been highly skilled in particular applications of their craft in their own country, and who content themselves with minor modifications of their technique to adapt to local conditions. These are the limited technologists. But the more effective person knows the general theory upon which the technology is based, and reinvents the technology in terms of local conditions. The theorist who can apply his theory is more adaptable than the rigidly practical man of limited horizons. Similarly, technologists from new nations are often sent abroad for training, and receive a highly detailed knowledge of a particular specialized modern application. But in five years' time this is likely to be out of date, and either they and their industry stagnate, or someone else must be sent once again to learn modern applications. Much more effective is the program which reinforces a man's theoretical knowledge, shows him how to apply it as a matter of dynamic re-evaluation, and shows him how to keep in touch with modern developments and the people who are innovating in the field, if not to innovate himself.

These observations can be generalized into the proposition that education will have greater impact on modernity if it is in applied general theory with an emphasis on technical mobility rather than a dependence upon periodic re-training.

There is one final point. Complete occupational mobility is neither practicable nor desirable. Further than this, modern economies are reaching the point where, with population expansion and automation, large sectors of the population may not be employable in the present conventional sense. To examine the implications of this would take us too far afield. But it must be stressed that our present patterns of mobility in the West should by no means be thought of as the ultimate development of occupational roles. Advanced countries as well as new nations may ultimately be faced with allowing for social roles for vast numbers of underemployed or nonemployed persons, devising equitable systems for providing them with an income, and amending our notions of reward and sanctions accordingly. For the West, with its still strongly entrenched Protestant ethic, this may be a most difficult experience to live through. For new nations, with their more relaxed approach to labor and to the dignity of man, the task may be much less difficult.

Adaptability of Organizations [5]

One of the most telling arguments against the bureaucratic form of modernity is that bureaucracies appear to be less adaptable than independent organizations. In particular, a department of government appears to be able to resist unorganized public pressure or opinion, in other words the wishes of the clients, for long periods of time. Relations between government departments seem frequently to be concerned with

[5] Cf. Amitai Etzioni, *Modern Organizations* (Englewood Cliffs, N.J.: Prentice-Hall, Inc., 1964) and references therein.

maintaining lines of authority and acting from motives of power or prestige. But these difficulties may be more apparent than real, since radical alterations of policy, the creation of new institutions, and the deletion of others, are common factors of political life.

The contemporary study of organizations, whether governmental or nongovernmental, is revealing regularities in their modes of adaptation, including methods of goal setting and internal adjustment. Most such studies have been structural or comparative in orientation, that is, they have seen organizations as complex self-bounded entities adjusting to external conditions by changing, expanding, or contracting their goals, and by rationalizing their internal modes of operation.

But insofar as they are elements in an economy or a system of social relations, organizations react upon one another. Two dimensions of this reaction, namely price competition and the integration of industrial processes, have been studied at length by economists. But a further dimension consists of the regularities of behavioral reaction as organizations become aware of the activities of others. Price cutting wars, cartels, monopoly agreements, enduring contracts creating binding relations and making provision for agreed reactions, partnerships and dissolutions are forms of organizational behavior which require sociological as well as economic or legal analysis. To what extent are these forms of interaction, and others like them, essential to the viability of the modern market economy? So far as I know a theory on this subject is not available for the guidance of new nations.

Boundaries in Social Structure

Under a previous heading an argument was presented in favor of mobility as a characteristic of a modern economy. It might be deduced from this that an economy with infinite mobility would be more modern, more advanced, than an economy with nil or limited mobility. However, all observed societies have a definable social structure, and social structure implies limitations on mobility.

Only two nonstructured, completely mobile societies can be envisaged. Neither has been observed empirically and neither is likely to be achieved except as limited enclaves within a wider structured society. One form would be primitive egalitarianism based on existing technical knowledge. This would be the complete interchangeability of roles irrespective of its technical consequences, and would imply complete self-sufficiency and lack of differentiated exchange, since differentiated exchange implies differentiation of social role. Such a society could not support complex technology and would have to do without its products or else import them from other societies. The second society is utopian communism, which would involve such an advance in automated production that humanity could withdraw from specialized relationships to machines, and distribution could be on the basis of need rather than earning power. While we may advance toward this much more than at present we can forecast, anything short of its complete attainment implies a social structure, even if that be nothing more than differences between caretakers of machines and the rest of society.

Almost all social structures are consistent with some form of economic growth, but not all are consistent with the requirements of modernity. Economic growth has taken place under the very different structural conditions of the United States, the U.S.S.R., France, Japan, India, Egypt, Venezuela, and Ghana. But only the first four countries meet the conditions of a fully modernized market economy, and even they have elements which do not share fully in the major activities of the economy as a whole (blighted and depressed areas in the United States, isolated ethnic groups or communities in the U.S.S.R. and Japan, some peasant areas of France). Once again we must stress the point that modernity is a comparative condition, not an absolute.

What we are concerned with in a modern economy is the nature of the interaction between the groups which can be identified as parts of the social structure. If it is possible for the groups to have complementary roles upon which modern market exchange can be based, if the communication between them is such that they react in support of each other's activities, and if their goals and actions are capable of modification to meet changing conditions, then the requirements of a modern economy can be met. From this point of view, the appearance of the formal paradigm of stratification is of less significance than the reality of relationships across group boundaries and the way in which groups adjust to new conditions.

To take an example, a class society can contain within it a myth of mobility. But in fact the rich industrial and commercial owners are likely to perpetuate their position and maintain it for their descendants, and directorates of the largest corporations are likely to be recruited from families which are already well established and wealthy, if for no other reason than that possession of money gives a man a capital advantage in maintaining the role ascribed to him. The effect of this may be leavened by actual recruitment of new wealthy families from other elements in society, and the myth of mobility may serve in addition to establish or reinforce an ethos of achievement among those who hold these roles.

Given such a set of factors, the consequences can be variable. The wealthy establishment may be flexible in its outlook, seeking new opportunities, prepared to switch its influence from banking to industry to government as the need arises, and to change its enterprises from family concerns to joint stock companies. This is not only in response to the economies of organization, but also to the ethos of the nation at large, including the views, aspirations, and purchasing desires of workers and other elements in society. This appears to be the case in the United States and is consistent with our criteria of modernity.

Or the wealthy establishment may be conservative and resist change, may be unaware of or contemptuous of the aspirations of other people, may lack a sense of production for others but only for themselves, to maintain their way of life. Under such conditions, boundaries are reinforced, reaction mechanisms are weakened, the economy is poorly articulated and static in outlook. This appears to be the case in some countries of Latin America, and to have been the case in Egypt.

It is quite possible for new nations to fall into this trap, and to ossify an elite in the form of a political junta supplemented by a few dependent industrialists. In a country such as India the situation is made more difficult because the effective caste system is nominally related to differences in occupation between castes. Yet for modernity to be achieved, new occupations must be introduced, and castes, if retained in fact, must develop unlikely flexibilities. It is possible for dual economies to emerge in forms analogous to that of Mexico in the first half of this century, that is with a vigorous urban life and a static, detached rural peasantry. If such solutions result in the new countries of, for example, Africa, modern economies will not exist, for exchange across social boundaries will be limited, formalized, and lack adaptability.

This should not, however, be taken for granted. In many new nations some of the new educated elite have been recruited from isolated rural peasantries. There are, it is true, ethnic or tribal groups which have dominated the educated classes and civil service, such as perhaps the Ibo of Nigeria. But within these tribal groups themselves there are vast differences of outlook now, and young men of other tribes are seeking their place in the sun. The reformation of the social structure will not settle down for many a decade, and it would be rash to predict its outcome with certainty.

Nevertheless, the condition remains. The economy will not be of modern viable form unless there is a flexible and effective interaction between the groups making up the social structure.

Information Flow

Communication, in the sense of a flow of information leading to reactions and feedback, is a technically significant element in a modern economy, so much so that it should perhaps be regarded as a factor of production.

Information is of many kinds. There is that which is integral to organization, providing a quick analysis of a stock or financial position, or the retrieval of data from records. Another kind consists of information of market conditions, the actions of competitors and suppliers, the reactions of customers and clients. A third consists of knowledge about technical and organizational innovations.

Such information permits an economy, and the elements within it, to react quickly and with maximum accuracy. Although in some form or another it has always existed, the years since World War II have seen the beginnings of a vast change in information systems, the effects of which are only just beginning to be felt. And it is only with this revolution that the specific importance of communication has come to be recognized, except as government propaganda services.

For such reasons, information services in the new nations are normally in a backward state and constitute a major inhibition to economic growth. At the crudest level, telephone and telegraph extend only to the major centers, and radio tends to be a one-way rather than a two-way system. Farmers and proprietors faced with this lack cannot be expected to react quickly to market conditions.

Similarly, the basic symbolic systems necessary to communication are poorly distributed or meet with serious blocks. Money is now usually well distributed, but is used in a real sense rather than a symbolic one, so that its application to many transactions is limited, and accounting is often crude. Linguistic and dialectical differences between social groups increase the distance between them, and despite the existence of a *lingua franca,* limit communication.

At a more sophisticated level, new nations lack a high development and wide distribution of such communications devices as credit rating bureaus, computers, or stock exchanges. To some extent they may be able to take advantage of new methods as they become economically feasible (for example, the electronic communication of library holdings over long distances from a central storage point), and this may enable them to move quickly into the most advanced modes. But the main obstacles to modernity in communications are likely to provide an insuperable barrier for several decades. These are the lack of an adequate distribution of education upon which a sophisticated symbol system must depend, and of specialized institutions to handle communication. The creation of institutions of this kind does not come easily to governments.

Physical Communications

By contrast, the importance of physical communications to move people and commodities has long been recognized. The opening up of sea routes to the East, the effect of macadamized roads and railways in Europe, the role of railways and wagon routes in the development of the West of North America, the influence of refrigerated shipping on Australia and New Zealand, are themes familiar to any economic historian. I myself have witnessed the sudden growth of cash marketing in a rural area of Fiji consequent upon one single change: the construction of a road which linked the rural farming area with market towns. Physical communications are significant both internationally and nationally.

Colonial governments did much to create a network of physical communications, but in Africa and much of Asia these were limited by two conditions which now have to be overcome if the economy is to modernize rapidly. One is that the international links were normally limited to those between the hinterland and the port of trade. There was little attempt to create regional networks between neighboring countries administered by different powers. Thus until very recently air travel between East and West Africa had to take place through Europe, and much telegraphic communication must follow this route even now.

The second is that internal communications were largely (though not wholly) determined either by administrative needs (linking administrative centers) or by European colonial definitions of economic strategy. Thus in Kenya, for example, roads were maintained to serve the white-settled Highlands, but they were not deliberately linked with any potential or designed peasant marketing system. Roads were designed to tap strategic sources of production, not to integrate an internal exchange system.

SOME CONDITIONS OF OPERATION

Achievement Orientation

One of the conditions frequently mentioned as being necessary to the character of a modern market economy is a high degree of orientation toward achievement. One form in which this characteristic is discussed is the presumed polarity between achieving and ascribing social roles. This we have already referred to at various points, and have concluded that social roles are usually attained and always maintained through a mixture of ascription and achievement, and that this is a feature of all societies, not just modern economies.

Another form of discussion centers around the achievement orientation of entrepreneurs. David C. McClelland, who has produced an extensive if controversial comparative study of this topic, defines achievement as "A desire to do well, not so much for the sake of social recognition or prestige, but to attain an inner feeling of accomplishment." [6] To distinguish between these two possible aspects of achievement is a matter of psychological technique, but to the sociologist or anthropologist a wide variety of motives would be legitimate. To link achievement to the inner feeling of accomplishment is difficult sociologically, and spreads achievement through almost every entrepreneurial act, and most other acts also, in all societies (the primitive artist, whether in pictorial, dance, or musical forms, is certainly achievement oriented; as is the agriculturalist who takes pride in his yams).

If achievement is the desire to do well, the sociologist and anthropologist would see it in many forms. Achievement is not absent from any society. How then can we compare them? McClelland's answer is to develop an index of the *degree* of achievement. Most sociologists and anthropologists, however, would focus upon the kind or quality of achievement before raising the question of degree. Western society appears to stress expansion and innovation in achievement in a manner which has not been present in many other societies, where achievement may consist in doing what has been prescribed, but doing it very well. This characteristic of Western achievement has grown substantially in the nineteenth and twentieth centuries, even in artistic fields. For the great artistic achievements have been the creation by the artist of new modes of statement. This is not typical of other societies, where the artist works within continuous conventions.

If Western achievement is expansive and innovative, the question remains, to what does it owe its existence? The nature of the Protestant ethic has been one source of explanation.[7] The expansion of Europe and the consequences for ethos and ultimately ideas, and then the education and socialization of children, has been another. In newly developing countries, one tends to look for the nonconformist, the man whose personal history has included such factors as rejection by his village, an idiosyncratic or minority religious upbringing, a traumatic separation from family through the death of parents or enforced schooling. Such

[6] David C. McClelland, "The Achievement Motive in Economic Growth," in B. F. Hoselitz and W. E. Moore, *Industrialization and Society* (Paris: Mouton, 1963), p. 76. See also McClelland's fuller work, *The Achieving Society* (Princeton, N.J.: D. Van Nostrand Co., Inc., 1961).

[7] Cf. Max Weber, *The Protestant Ethic and the Spirit of Capitalism* (New York: Charles Scribner's Sons, 1958); and Kurt Samuelsson, *Religion and Economic Action* (London: William Heinemann, Ltd., 1961).

factors throw a man back on his own resources, give him a detached and manipulative view of society, and are often linked with a quasi-fanatic devotion to achievement. These are merely indications of possible origins of relevant achievement, a question which needs a great deal of further detailed study.

Security, Predictability, and Tension

It is becoming increasingly evident that an economy with an expansive orientation cannot operate unless both security (and predictability) and tension are present. The model here is very similar to the psychological model of need-satisfaction, the biological model of homeostasis, and the economic model of equilibrium. Unless there are unsatisfied wants, and unless there are ideas and conditions which create more dissatisfaction, there will be no action, and this becomes more critical in an expansive economy than in a static one. The mode of action is more often than not to seek a regularity of solution which is the search for predictability and security: only some innovators are exceptions to this rule.

The search for security in the modern economy is additionally expressed in two dimensions. Nationally, there is a desire for political certainty and predictability of the law. The business community frequently does not mind whether a political system is totalitarian or democratic, as long as it is stable and protects commercial transactions. At the individual or firm level, the search for security expresses itself in modern forms of prestation (expense accounts and gifts), in contracts, and in partnerships or cartels.

Institutionalized Services

Among the conditions for the operation of a modern economy are the effective existence of a number of organized services which are often not present, or present with substantial defects, in underdeveloped countries. Among these are the record-keeping, communication, and transportation services mentioned previously.

In addition, warehousing and storage facilities are often of significance, particularly as they may affect a possible growth in sophistication of peasant marketing. Credit and banking institutions, while present now in all countries, are usually confined to the already sophisticated sector of the economy, and while credit unions have been experimented with they do not usually have the resources to feed productive capital into those parts of the economy which require modernization. Most government loan funds are of necessity administered in such a way that the peasant cannot provide the security that is needed to obtain money, or the system of credit ratings is so poor that there is a high rate of loss. There is still room for considerable innovation in the institutions distributing capital, and economies will have difficulty modernizing unless such innovation takes place.

Finally, modern economies depend to a very great extent upon the existence of a skilled labor force, which in turn depends upon a widespread and effective system of technical education, whether administered through firms themselves or through institutes and schools. Newly developing nations are rightly putting great emphasis upon this strategic activity in an endeavor to make up the gaps in the colonial educational systems they inherited.

THE DYNAMIC ORIENTATION

Most of the conditions so far discussed in this chapter would apply to a technically advanced but stationary economy. Yet the most dramatic characteristic of modern economies, which provides both a challenge and an almost overwhelming difficulty for new nations, is that they have a rapid growth rate: they are dynamically oriented. The discussion has touched upon this at one or two points, especially with regard to entrepreneurs and achievement, but we must now examine the conditions of growth more fully.

Expansion Motivation

One factor in economic growth is the manner in which motivations and institutional arrangements combine to provide the interest in expansion. This theme can be followed through two processes, production and consumption.

A. O. Hirschman refers to the former theme as the "need for built-in spurs" to maintain the level of achievement and expansive interest of the individual firm.[8] He lists a revealing set of common defects in firms in underdeveloped countries which show the many ways in which the requisite spurs can be absent.

1. Absence of a sufficiently vigorous "growth mentality" reflected in:
   a. failure to plow back profits adequately, tendency toward "milking" firms;
   b. failure to keep up with technological progress abroad;
   c. preference for a stagnating enterprise that stays "within the family" over expansion that is bought at the cost of partial surrender of control.

[8] Hirschman, *The Strategy of Economic Development,* Chap. 8.

2. Difficulties in administration, management, and "human relations," shown in such symptoms as:
   a. excessive centralization of decision making and inability or unwillingness to delegate authority;
   b. ineffective staff work and coordination;
   c. failure to pay adequate salaries to key personnel in spite of high turnover and recognized scarcity;
   d. failure to impart to subordinates a feeling of participation and spirit of initiative;
   e. neglect of personal relations and morale;
   f. neglect of public relations.
3. Difficulties in carrying out functions not directly connected with the central production process, evidenced in:
   a. defective advance planning (engineering studies, market research, provision for finance);
   b. defective cost accounting and control in general;
   c. defective maintenance.

Hirschman points out that such defects are frequently found in advanced countries, so that the matter resolves itself into one of empirical examination and comparative effectiveness. Clearly too, these defects are not always present, and it is sometimes difficult to judge what the situation may be.

With regard to 1a, for example, I have observed very primitive entrepreneurial beginnings in New Guinea, in which the production and consumption elements in a boat-building and copra marketing enterprise were inextricably mixed. A normal examination of accounts would show "milking" for personal consumption. Yet that personal consumption (parties and gifts included) was used to generate labor output, and the result was an overall expansion and growing complexity of production and organization.

And with regard to 1c, I have observed an analogous situation in Fiji, in which a native manganese production enterprise refused to permit an advanced Western sleeping partner to take over technical production, introduce heavy capital equipment, and expand output several-fold. Among the reasons why the takeover was refused was the prediction that the Western firm would work out the deposit rapidly at a time of low prices, even taking a loss on the production side, in order to make a profit on the trading operation. The Fijians wanted a slow rate of production giving them an opportunity to balance low prices against high ones, with a steady rate of income over a number of years which they could absorb and use as capital to establish a wider range of enterprises. From the point of view of an immediate result on the colony's overall growth figures, the Western firm was right. But from the point of view of a long-term result building up local enterprise and initiative, the Fijians were right.

I mention these points, not to dispute the validity of Hirschman's list, but to indicate that the decision as to whether an act belongs in it or not, and the judgment as to its effects on growth, is not always straightforward.

The second set of spurs are consumption spurs. The assumption of Western economics is that man has an infinity of wants, the more he obtains the more he desires, and production cannot keep up with demand. This assumption is not always true, but it is a necessary base for economic growth.

The pattern and scale of consumption are cultural facts, the resultant of all the forces which bear upon the total culture: the anthropologist's cultural pattern and the economist's demand schedule are in fact the same thing, although in describing them anthropologist and economist use different methods of weighting and analysis. In some societies, rapidly diminishing in number, cultural horizons are so limited that the range of wants is finite. As new possibilities are introduced into the culture, they are adopted as single items or trait complexes without having any multiplying effect on the economy.

Such introductions have two effects. One is that change, when it occurs, is of a step-by-step nature from one consumption pattern to another, without contributing to dynamic modernity. Such was the case in many colonial areas prior to World War II. Secondly, it introduces the likelihood of a fixed ceiling on income requirements. There is only so much tobacco that a man can smoke, and in nonliterate peasant conditions, only so much need for kerosene, and in the tropics only a limited requirement for cloth. Individuals expend effort to reach that level of income, and when it is reached, stop working.

The change to dynamic infinite wants comes about as consumption patterns with multiplying effects are introduced, when possibilities exist of reaching the consumption of expensive items, and when education and contact with the Western world reveal the potentiality of reaching a wide range of consumer goods. Roads, for example, have a multiplying effect, leading to a demand for more and better roads, and the vehicles to use on them, from bicycles to lorries. Schools, if backed by a supply of literature, and if beyond a minimal educational standard, also have a multiplying effect, leading to a demand for more educational facilities, and for such things as books and magazines and radio programs.

The study of the effects of differing types of consumption, and relations between consumption and income, was an early interest of both sociology and economics, but has declined in intensity and effectiveness over the past few decades. In a recent article, however, Simon Kuznets has made some further observations on consumption patterns which may stimulate further analysis of this strategic topic.[9]

First, he introduces qualifications to the familiar theme that as income grows patterns of consumption change. He shows, by international comparisons, that developed countries spend a higher proportion of their income on government expenditure than do underdeveloped countries, and a higher proportion of capital as contrasted with consumption, although the differences are not as great as one might expect. On a straight money-expenditure basis underdeveloped countries spend a much higher proportion of their consumption expenditure on food than do the richer nations, and much less on such items as transportation, recreation, and furniture. But these ratios change very much if we correct the figures to allow for price differences between countries: under these circumstances, the differences in proportions of income spent on food become much smaller. This type of analysis is still difficult to control comparatively, but Kuznets' approximations are bound to be refined and lead to more subtle results.

More significantly, perhaps, Kuznets suggests a distinction between two types of consumption expenditure. Required components of consumption are those upon which capital formation and increased productivity are based, thus leading directly toward growth. Thus basic food maintains the population at a healthy level, enabling it to perform efficiently as a work force. Discretionary components are consumption items which, if foregone, would not reduce the effectiveness of the economic system in a growth orientation. Kuznets gives as an example expenditure on certain types of amusement (without defining them).

There is a similarity here in style of analysis with the familiar category of necessary social expenditures, for example on technical education and health services, which are essential to the performance of a modern economy, and other social expenditures, such as on concert halls, which are sometimes deemed not to have the same effect.

Such categories need much greater refinement before they can account accurately for consumption effects on the production system through the ramifications of exchange. Is it true or false that all consumption needs spur men to effort, to exchange their income for them, and to produce more to earn the requisite income? If this statement is true, how then do we distinguish between one category of consumption

[9] Simon Kuznets, "Consumption, Industrialization and Urbanization," in B. F. Hoselitz and W. E. Moore, eds., *Industrialization and Society* (Paris: UNESCO and Mouton, 1963), pp. 99-115.

and another? Does consumption merely divert income from capital use, or does it, by stimulating exchange, create more sources of profit, hence more capital?

What we need to do with more objectivity is to examine the multiplying effects and ramifications of given acts of consumption with a view to determining their effects on the system as a whole. When a man engages in a traditional ceremony as its principal, how much productive effort does he thereby stimulate in others? In the process of accumulating the requisite goods and services, to what extent does exchange take place with profit taking, and to what extent does that profit taking serve as a capital basis for additional activity? In other words, to what extent is the given ceremonial a spur to growth? Too often we answer such questions on a moral basis, holding that certain acts of consumption are luxuries as against necessities, or are morally wasteful, or do not fit in with our notion of a Western middle-class Protestant ethic. But these are very different questions from asking what are the effects of ceremony, beer drinking, religious and charitable support, operas, and football on the scale, complexity, articulation, and growth orientation of the economic system?

Investment

If all members of a society passed on to the succeeding generation the same quantity of capital equipment, merely maintaining it without expansion or diminution, and if the population remained steady, the only possibility of improving the per capital level of income would be through additional work or an improved organization. If the additional work involved an improvement of skills, it would be regarded as a result of a nonmaterial form of investment, namely education or training. So, too, we could regard an improvement in organization, for investment is essentially using resources to improve man's stock of resources, and improved organization is the result of using knowledge and ideas (resources) to create a new tool in the shape of new and continuous modes of doing things.

Since the amount of physical labor available is strictly limited by both physiological and cultural considerations, it follows that a major element in the capacity of an economy to grow is its ability to invest. This point is usually well understood for modern economies, but is frequently overlooked in ecological interpretations of primitive societies. The nature of Eskimo, Polynesian, or Kwakiutl economy is affected not merely by imperatives of the environment, but by tools (social as well as material) which were available to the people to exploit that environment.

Sociologically, investment thus covers an enormous range of creative human behavior. It begins with the state of knowledge, and as a technical matter, is essentially the process of cumulative cultural change or innovation. It must be recognized, of course, that not all cultural change is cumulative, in the sense of adding to resources, since there are instances of the decline of civilizations.

If we think technologically rather than financially, the rate of investment is the rate of innovation together with the rate at which innovations spread through the relevant parts of the economy, which may be termed the rate of diffusion. Both the rate of innovation and that of diffusion are linked less with personality variables in the society than with motivations and opportunities for expansion. They are thus dependent upon rewards and costs, both in material terms, and in the form of a congruence with ethical, aesthetic, and similar judgments. These determine the degree of probability that innovation will be sought.

To the extent that innovation is sought, other conditions influence the likelihood of its occurring and diffusing. One is what might be termed the quantity of ideas in the cultural pool. A very few innovations appear to be based upon chance discovery. But for the discovery to be valid, it must be seen to be relevant, that is, it must be related to pre-existing knowledge so that it may be interpreted and applied. The chances of this happening in fact will be greater, the greater and better organized the pre-existing set of knowledge. More important, most innovations come about through the rearrangement of existing elements of knowledge, the rearrangement itself becoming something new. The more knowledge becomes sophisticated and self-consciously expanding, the more significant expansion by rearrangement becomes. The number of possible permutations and recombinations, and thus the chances of new knowledge developing, is very much greater when the pool of ideas from which the innovators can draw is greater. This is one of the major reasons for the tremendous speed-up in technical innovation in the twentieth century, a speed-up which is continuing at an ever-increasing rate.

Another condition is the degree of mobility and flexibility in the society itself. If the stratification system or power interests are concerned with maintaining a status quo, or if villagers are afraid of new ideas and actions because of the personal risks and insecurities involved, or if the resource base does not lend itself, because of property rights or the very fact of poverty, to change, then the flow of new ideas (which may come from outside) may merely be a disturbing irritant rather than a stimulus to change and investment. It may be argued that a major factor contributing to growth through effective investment in the United States is the very high degree of mobility and flexibility evident in such matters as changing fashions, occupational changes, and geographical migration.

But investment in the modern economy is expressed not merely through technical innovation but also through the financial mechanism. The ability to engage in technical innovation is very frequently linked with the ability to buy the resources necessary for the innovation, or to call the production of a new machine into being by contracting to buy it, or to defer income and sales until re-tooling has taken place. Such acts imply a control over financial capital which can be used for these purposes.

In order to gain significant quantities of financial capital from their own operations, underdeveloped countries are faced with the task of stimulating the earning of income, some of which can be diverted from direct consumption to a savings pool. It is at least doubtful, however, whether this will increase or decrease the availability of capital in the long run. If the deferred consumption would have been spent largely on imported commodities, it could contribute to a detrimental balance of payments problem with overseas countries. But if it would have been spent on internal local industry, it would have contributed to the increased division of labor, the growth of production institutions, and an increased volume of transactions. It would thus have contributed to the second source of capital accumulation, namely profit taking.

In some respects, profit taking is more important as a dynamic for newly growing economies than personal savings. For it is frequently the case that personal savings are merely hoarded, for example in the form of jewelry in Malaysia, and are thus nonproductive. Further, many personal savers do so primarily to spend on consumption goods rather than to increase investment. On the other hand the firm or individual interested in profit taking is also liable to be interested in using capital for further expansion. Hence it might be argued that savings in the hands of entrepreneurs leads to greater investment than personal savings, unless the institutions mobilize and channel personal savings (through banks or lending) for the use of entrepreneurs. This is a matter of cultural values, institutional arrangements, and social structure.

If this is the case, a major factor in stimulating productive capital accumulation will be the degree of division of labor between industrial and commercial units and the velocity of exchange between them. For every act of exchange provides an opportunity for profit taking, and profit taking is the source of capital.

But there is another factor with sociological implications to be considered. This is the available quantity of money in relation to the quantity of transactions to be serviced by it. The importance of this factor is borne out by such generalizations as the following. If the quantity of money is low, it will keep money prices low and make it more difficult to take a substantial profit. If the quantity of money is high, it will be easier to borrow substantial sums for new capital investment. Whereas rapid inflation has seriously disturbing effects on an economy, primarily because it is uneven in its spread and effects, mild inflation can imply that the money supply is running ahead of the supply of goods and services, is readily available for capital expansion, and is a stimulus to production, since expenditure at a time of low prices will bring results in times of higher prices.

But the available quantity of money consists not only of the physical coinage in circulation, but also of the amount of credit which is provided as a book entry. Currency control is affected by various banking devices, such as relating the physical currency to a stock of gold which it is supposed to equate in value, or to given forms of overseas exchange funds, or by limiting the amount of bank credit to certain reserves which the banks must hold.

Fundamentally, these limitations link with two requirements of a banking system in a modern economy. One is that it be controllable in the interests of the national well-being. The other is that money must continue to be exchangeable, and this is a matter of confidence. The national public is more likely to retain its confidence in money if it is linked with something tangible and real in these ways, and the currency is more likely to retain its international exchangeability if its value is kept within certain limits of fluctuation. To the extent that confidence in the currency is retained, there is every possibility that the supply of physical currency and credit could increase considerably, if not indefinitely, provided that the economic consequences of such an increase was desirable.

We are, I think, entering a phase in Western economies which involves a considerable change in attitudes towards money as a symbol and as a source of credit. The widespread growth of the use of personal credit since World War II, and the simultaneous growth of personal checking and credit cards, together with the beginnings of an acceptance of computers and a decline in public interest in such physical criteria as the gold standard, have all contributed to the increased interpretation of money as the symbol of purchasing power. This will inevitably increase the flexibility of the public reaction to monetary manipulation.

More than that, the issuance of credit becomes a form of investment, postpaid rather than prepaid as was the case with savings. Although it has the obvious danger that it can cause a sharp retrenchment of expenditure suddenly when a credit ceiling is reached, it can nevertheless have an advantage for maintaining an economic dynamic. The older forms of saving (still of course very widespread) tended to withdraw funds from circulation for the saving period (this being partially counter-balanced by the lending of the saved amount), but the supply of credit can increase the amount and velocity of circulation. The ability to invest is now less a matter of double waiting (waiting while saving and then waiting until the capital creates a return) than of obtaining credit.

Insofar as this is true, it has some important consequences. Most countries of the world have for some time been experiencing rapid population increase. It may indeed be questioned as to whether this population increase provided the dynamic in Western countries which kept the postwar damage replacement boom in operation and converted it into what appears to be a predictably continuous period of growth.

In any event the population increase in the West would of itself have little effect on the economy unless it could be translated into increased purchasing power, at a time indeed when automation is beginning to reduce the demand for certain forms of labor. Whereas in the nineteenth century it is probable that the requirements of young adults would have been met by penurious saving, with the acceptance of an initial low level of living and minimal consumption effect on the economy, the requirements today are largely met by borrowing, with a demand for an initial level of living (in terms of housing, education, cars, and children) inconceivable in earlier generations. Only the widespread use of credit, with its implied confidence in the symbol of money and the continuation of purchasing power, would make this possible at present levels.

New nations are at a considerable disadvantage in this regard. Unfortunately, most of them are dependent on export staples for a flow of imports essential to their basic growth. If they were isolated and self-sufficient, a liberal internal credit policy, growing as confidence in and experience with money increased, might do much to meet their own problems of population growth and to stimulate a diversity of production. But such a policy is liable to be inflationary and to decrease the amount of imports which can be bought with a given amount of exports.

Whether internal or international credit systems can be devised which can meet the needs of new nations with minimal balance of payments and inflationary consequences is a major problem for economic ingenuity.

Continuity and Tension

The process of economic growth is based upon a permanent or protracted condition in which there is a margin between action and the satisfaction of new wants. As one schedule of wants comes close to be satisfied it is replaced by another which serves to organize additional activity. This implies that culture, and the society associated with it, is in change: economic growth and sociocultural change towards an increased order of complexity are different ways of looking at the same thing.

However, change can be disruptive and can dislocate the pre-existing system, particularly if its origin lies in factors outside the system.[10] Over most of the world we can observe relatively small discrete social systems in rural societies adjusting to the impact of the formation of national polities and economies. Sometimes the rural systems can maintain a continuity by minimizing the links with the wider society. This appears, for example, to be the case for much of the Mediterranean area despite the turmoil of the centuries following the decline of Greece and Rome.[11] A conservative continuity is preserved in significant sectors despite the rapid change of the wider society. The articulation is sufficient for a result based upon unsolved tensions; the continuity is a permanent state of strain which, when minor, can be incorporated into a way of life, or, when major, is a condition of demoralizing anomie.

More usually, we assume that the harsh disruption which has come about in many parts of Asia, Africa, and Oceania will ultimately correct itself through the formation of new societies which can be conceived of as operating units.

This question conceals a number of built-in value premises, which are important to our analysis. Our conception of a society or an economy is one with articulated self-correcting parts. But some societies may not be like this, and many of interest to the future might conceivably continue, but in a static sense, as a congeries of relatively discrete units. There is nothing inevitable about the creation or the continuation of articulated societies.

Nevertheless we cannot conceive of modern economic growth without continuous articulation, that is the continuity of the social system. But the precise meaning of this is, at the moment, a matter of judgment. It cannot mean a society in perfect balance, in perfect equilibrium, for if that were the case there would not be the ever-changing demand pattern which creates the tension necessary for new action. Hirschman, indeed, argues cogently that a lack of balance in the components of a society is the driving force for social reform and for economic change, and hence economic growth is most likely to be rapid under such conditions.

But there must be at least a minimal articulation and organization, or

[10] See particularly, Godfrey and Monica Wilson, *The Analysis of Social Change* (Cambridge: Cambridge University Press, 1954).

[11] Cf. Julian Pitt-Rivers, ed., *Mediterranean Countrymen* (Paris: Mouton, 1963).

the tension will be so great as to be disruptive, and there will be marked discontinuities [12] of social experience holding up the overall movement of the economy. Just what the difference is between pathological disruption and stimulating or beneficial tension in a society or economy has not yet been cogently or satisfactorily reasoned. The problem is intimately bound up with the question of the continuity of society or the transformation of one society into another. Empirically, it is closely linked with the ability of the power elite in a national society to transform its values and operations as circumstances dictate, and of the inhabitants of rural villages to secure the social and economic reforms or altered conditions to making their striving worthwhile.

Population Distribution

Examples of the way in which many of the preceding factors operate can be seen in some of the phenomena of population distribution, interpreted widely.

The distribution of population between aged dependents, productive workers, and growing generations of children is frequently interpreted in terms of the direct effects upon productivity and the uses of production. In other words, such distributions indicate a great deal about whether income has to be used for welfare purposes, or whether it can be used for immediate productive efforts. They link too with comparisons between the present and the future. Can, for example, the low income of parents now be justified because it will result in a well-trained numerous labor force as present children enter it in the future.

Between the direct numerical data and the reality lie many assumptions. The U.S.S.R. requires a great deal of direct state expenditure for the comfort of the aged as a postponed reward of labor, whereas some primitive societies seek a small but nevertheless continuous output from the aged. In connection with training, it may be that the expenditures of the parental generation are largely vitiated by a transformation of technical requirements: training can be for the past rather than the future.

A major element in a potential dynamic force is whether the young develop new ideas by comparison with those of their parents, and whether, if so, they have the opportunity to translate them into action. Primitive societies are characterized by the continuous replacement of one generation by another with much the same wants and values. In dynamic societies the socialization process is imperfect and, added to

[12] See Neil Smelser, *The Sociology of Economic Life* (Englewood Cliffs, N.J.: Prentice-Hall, Inc., 1963), pp. 112-15.

the complexity of the pool of ideas, makes possible transformations over time.

Another possible force emerges from the distribution of the population between an urban and a rural way of life, and the interlinkages between them. Not all cities are dynamic or growth oriented, but the type of urbanization familiar to students of the twentieth century is. Over the past century or so it has been in the towns that industry has located (there is a small trend away from this in some areas now), so that urbanization and industrialization have become more or less synonymous. Moreover the urban way of life has been characterized by a continuous search for improvement, and an intellectual excitement derived from the intense interplay of ideas.

So much has this been the case that writers such as Colin Clark, and those who have modified his position such as Harvey Leibenstein, have been able to show that the most rapidly growing economies are the ones with the highest proportion of population in the cities.[13] Interpretations derived from this relationship need careful formulation. But among them we have the probability that the growth of industrial urban centers (as distinct from commercial or administrative entrepôts) made possible the industrial dynamic we know today, through the concentration of capital, the presence of a differentiated labor force, and the growth of ideas, skills, and motivations. This in turn made possible many of the technical advances which could be applied to agriculture, and as time went on, permitted the application of increased capital to agriculture. But in turn, this would only have been possible with the removal of the agricultural population from the land to the towns, since the process of migration removed many who were not skilled as farmers, since greater use of capital was more effective on larger farming units, and since the towns provided the market for the increased agricultural production.

Insofar as these relationships hold good, new nations would probably be well advised to encourage the growth of towns as a major impetus for economic growth and agricultural reform.

Movement of population from the countryside to the city has an uncomfortable side effect, namely making evident the disadvantages of underemployment, which is often hidden in the villages but which cannot be hidden in the towns. However, an underemployed villager is likely to be preventing his neighbor from using resources to occupy himself fully, and in the relatively undifferentiated countryside will have few opportunities to find alternative outlets for his skills. In the cities there

---

[13] Colin Clark, *The Conditions of Economic Progress* (London: Macmillan & Co., Ltd., 1957); Harvey Leibenstein, *Economic Backwardness and Economic Growth* (New York: John Wiley & Sons, Inc., 1957).

is the probability, provided management and capital are available, that under- or unemployment will make it possible for new industries to emerge.

Movement between village and city is but one example, perhaps the most important one, of mobility in the geographical distribution of population. But the consideration remains that in many countries the cities which have grown up are in some instances the wrong ones for the twentieth century. They are located in areas of economic stagnation or decline, propped up by artificial aids and subsidies. Increasingly, Western countries are learning to encourage the geographical mobility of labor at all levels, managerial and manual, rather than tying down the economy to particular locations of endeavor. This is a major characteristic of the United States which appears to be of increasing significance, and the growth of the European Common Market and agreements flowing from it have made possible the movement of labor from one country to another among all the participating members.

Here again is a difficulty for new nations; for geographical mobility is hampered by the weakness of rewards, by the lack of differentiation in the labor force, and by tribal and similar frictions in the social structure.

COMPLEXITY

If one were to identify the social properties of an exchange system or market economy which was highly modernized, or at an advanced stage of development by comparison with others, we might do so by reference to its complexity. For the performance of an economy appears to depend very largely on the scale of the resources it can handle, which in turn is a function of technological efficiency and organization. Both are affected by the state of the cultural pool of ideas, and organization within the economy is connected with the social division of labor and the exchange system which links the component parts together. Although it is possible to have a division of labor, both as to knowledge and action, which is overspecialized, in that it is beyond the capacity of the individuals playing the roles to interact with optimum efficiency, it is nevertheless generally true that economic development demands an increasing diversification of roles. The quantity of organized ideas and the diversity of roles coordinated through organization and the exchange system constitute the complexity of society which is correlated with a particular degree of economic development.

This in fact has been the short way of stating the problem of those countries which are consciously striving to modernize their economy. We have identified some essential functions of modernity (for example, the value of transportation or of symbolic communication), but we have done so, on the whole, in analytical terms rather than by proselytizing for any particular ethnic solution. Communism may be better or worse than capitalism, and the new nations may create social systems which are neither. Some elements in the capitalist system may be demonstrably more efficient than some in a communist system, and vice versa, but this must be demonstrated on its own merits in relation to a particular social and economic context.

We do not demand a priori that ceremonial exchange must give way in the course of modernization: this must depend upon the nature of the ceremonial, its consequences and ramifications, and whether it can be harnessed to a dynamic. But we do demand as a condition of modernization such features as an achievement orientation directed toward expansion, and a complexity of exchange relationships.

Whether people decide to emphasize the consumption of betel nut, rather than scotch whiskey, to have a polygynous household rather than a monogamous one, to train witch doctors rather than psychiatrists, or to spend wealth on medical services rather than opera, is of itself of no concern in the analysis of the exchange system or of economic growth. Too often judgments about the viability of an economy (or of a social system for that matter) are based upon judgments about the moral or ethical appropriateness of patterns of consumption. We would prefer such judgments to be based rather upon an analysis of the complexity and operation of the exchange system, and of the social organization and culture upon which it rests.

INDEX